BIBLICAL MISSIONS

Workbook

BIBLICAL MISSIONS
Workbook

PRINCIPLES,

PRIORITIES,

AND PRACTICES

MARK TATLOCK AND
CHRIS BURNETT, EDS.

THOMAS NELSON®
Since 1798

THOMAS NELSON

Biblical Missions Workbook

Copyright © 2025 by The Master's Academy International

Published in Nashville, Tennessee, by Thomas Nelson. Thomas Nelson is a registered trademark of HarperCollins Christian Publishing, Inc.

Thomas Nelson titles may be purchased in bulk for educational, business, fundraising, or sales promotional use. For information, please email SpecialMarkets@ThomasNelson.com.

ISBN 978-0-310-15818-9 (Softcover)
ISBN 978-0-310-15828-8 (eBook)

Cover design: Maffrine LaConte

Printed in the United States of America

24 25 26 27 28 PHP 5 4 3 2 1

CONTENTS

INTRODUCTION TO THE
BIBLICAL MISSIONS WORKBOOK

When it comes to global missions, the separation of theory from practice can be a matter of life and death. For students learning a new topic or deepening their knowledge in a discipline, theory and practice can seem impossibly distant from each other. Concepts can seem out of touch from real life—as high up as an ivory tower—while actions on the ground might dismiss well-researched "best practices" altogether.

The *Biblical Missions Workbook* seeks to make biblical missions actionable. Twenty-four lessons follow the outline of the *Biblical Missions: Principles, Priorities, and Practices* textbook. The lessons serve as companion guides for real-life application of the textbook's biblical teaching on a wide variety of missions subjects. Thus, terms that can be found in the textbook's glossary are boldfaced in the workbook's first use of them to aid student learning and navigation between the two volumes. The goal of each lesson is to help the user understand and apply basic knowledge in personal and practical ways, no longer as a reader but as a student. Complexity builds as each lesson develops, so that students have new tools for implementing biblically trustworthy ideas in God-glorifying actions in any global context.

How to Use the Workbook

The *Biblical Missions Workbook* is unique in that it provides a storehouse of missions-related questions and project ideas that both students and instructors of all types can utilize as ready curriculum for any class setting. The abundance of questions and prompts within each lesson allows for selectivity as to which questions are asked and answered and which projects are assigned. For use in a course or Bible study, teachers are encouraged to assign what will best suit their audience, their learning outcomes, and the student's time availability and capacity to access resources online or in a library. The flexible design of the workbook ensures that everyone will benefit from all sections of the lessons, according to their situation.

The Audience of the Workbook

Now that you have opened this workbook, you are no longer a reader but a student! The lessons are designed with you in mind, either as a "leader" or a "learner," both of which are workbook student categories. The distinctions are meant to reflect your relationship to others within the environments in which you will use the workbook: ecclesiastical (local church), institutional (school), or organizational (sending, training, and field agencies). You will find yourself in the following table according to your role in the environment in which you complete the workbook lessons.

	Ecclesiastical (Local Churches)	Institutional (Academic Programs)	Organizational (Agencies and Fields)
Leaders	Pastors and lay leaders	Faculty and administration	Executives and field leaders
Learners	Members, including those in missions training	Students, including those of missiology or in missions training	Missionaries, candidates, and trainees

Seeing yourself as a student in relationship to others in your target environment should encourage you to use the workbook in a group setting, if possible. Here are some examples of group participation that would benefit you and others as you learn more about biblical missions:

- *Ecclesiastical*: church equipping classes moderated by an elder or lay leader; home group Bible study; discipleship and missionary candidate training
- *Institutional*: for-credit missions or missiology curriculum; interdisciplinary use of the readings, projects, and assignments by courses in business, linguistics, history, social studies, Bible and theology, or other fields
- *Organizational*: continuing education courses for agency directors and staff or field leaders and their teams; training program material for candidates, trainees, and donors; assessment tool for investigating and reviewing a missionary's doctrine, philosophy of ministry, and activities

Understanding the Workbook Categories

Textbook Content

The first page of all twenty-four lessons has the same layout. At the top of the sidebar is a concise view of the textbook material covered in the workbook lesson. Every question and project prompt in the lesson is derived from the textbook entries. The workbook is not randomly selected but follows the textbook sequentially and corresponds to a subsection or section in the textbook. Students are encouraged to consult the textbook entries as they answer the workbook questions.

Summary of Textbook Content

Each lesson provides a synopsis of the key themes discussed in the textbook material, which then serves as an introduction and overview of what follows in the workbook.

Learning Objectives

Before any questions are asked, a list of learning objectives is provided, which sets the stage for the learning to come. The list explains what students can expect in the workbook lesson as well as what they should be able to reproduce by the end of the lesson.

Key Memory Verse

On the first page of each lesson, a Bible passage is listed that best captures the thrust of the lesson and the material covered in the textbook. Below this verse are Additional Memory Verses and Scriptures for Further Meditation, which students are encouraged to commit either to memory or to devotional study.

Recall and Reflect

The questions included in the Recall and Reflect section are intended to foster basic comprehension based on the initial review of the textbook material. They may be completed with a simple short-answer response. For this category, only citations to the corresponding chapters and inserts of the textbook are provided for each question to aid students' initial familiarization and overview of the textbook material being studied.

Analyze

The questions included in the Analyze section are intended to foster critical analysis of the textbook material. Here students are encouraged to think more deeply on missions issues. While questions in this category remain connected to the textbook material, students must think beyond what the textbook authors have written and engage with the material at a higher level.

Implement

The questions included in the Implement section are intended to promote personal development through actionable steps that are derived directly from the textbook material. These application-oriented questions encourage students to put the knowledge they just acquired into action.

Ask a Missionary

The Ask a Missionary category provides an opportunity to engage with former or current missionaries about the themes presented in the textbook material to understand their views and learn from their experiences. It has the goal of stimulating missionary preparation and outlook for candidates and trainees as well as providing an accountability tool for sending churches, supporters, and missions leadership. We encourage students to take these questions into a face-to-face conversation, if possible, and to write in their answers to the workbook afterward.

Study the Scriptures

The questions included in the Study the Scripture section are intended to encourage interaction with the biblical texts on the theme of the textbook material. This category is best used devotionally, as discussion questions for a group Bible study or teaching opportunity, or as an aid to pastors, teachers, or missionaries in the sermon preparation process.

Missions Research

The Missions Research section provides prompts that encourage further investigation into missions-related topics, many of which are context-specific. Workbook users from all student categories are encouraged to attempt the prompts to the best of their ability, leveraging internet and library research, books, magazines, journals, news outlets, interviews, debates, conferences, and seminars, among other resources. While every lesson includes widely accessible prompts, the rationale behind the more involved research prompts is to challenge all who are ready for deeper missions investigations, such as leaders, trainers, and those being trained for ministries requiring ordination. Many of these prompts can be implemented in course projects and assignments, and many will require the use of additional paper or personal computer.

Application Projects

The Application Projects are prompts with actionable steps that serve as personal projects that students can undertake individually or with a group. Some prompts are for practical research into a context of a student's choosing, while others aim to produce deliverables (e.g., sermons, presentations, activities, assessments) for the students' church or ministry, present or future. Still other prompts draw together several concepts and might constitute comprehensive assessment assignments for students in missions courses and training programs. Our hope is that some of the practical work of the Application Projects will result in ministry adjustments and new designs by individuals and teams. As with missions research prompts, many application projects will require additional paper or a personal computer.

Special Thanks

The *Biblical Missions Workbook* is the product of many hands and hearts. We, the general editors, have regularly given thanks to God for the following teammates and desire to publicly acknowledge them for the prayerful gratitude of all workbook students: Josiah Sisto, editorial project manager; Collin Vassallo, lead designer, writer, and team manager; Tony LaConte, writer; copy editors Joshua Sherrill and Jamie Bissmeyer; Hillary Megee, concept designer; Max Megee, curriculum consultant; early contributors Adam Wilson, Will Hale, and Bien Cedro; and Maffrine LaConte, cover designer. We echo Paul's sentiment in Philippians 1:3–5: "I thank my God in all my remembrance of you, always offering prayer with joy in my every prayer for you all, because of your fellowship in the gospel from the first day until now."

First Steps to the Field

Biblical Authority and Sufficiency

Textbook Content

CHAPTER 1: Fidelity to the Word of God in Missions: Scripture as the Launch, Life, and Legacy of the First Missionaries, by Abner Chou

    INSERT 1.1: Trends in Global Missions Away from Biblical Fidelity, by E. D. Burns

CHAPTER 2: The Authority and the Sufficiency of the Bible for the Missionary Task, by Chris Burnett

    INSERT 2.1: Missiological Application: God-Ordained Authority in Missions, by Mark Tatlock

    INSERT 2.2: The Influence of African Authority Structures on Spirituality, by Nathan Odede

CHAPTER 3: A Biblical View of God's Servants, Work, and the Church, by David Doran

Key Memory Verse

All Scripture is God-breathed and profitable for teaching, for reproof, for correction, for training in righteousness.

—2 TIMOTHY 3:16

Additional Memory Verses

- 1 Corinthians 1:18–24
- 1 Thessalonians 2:4
- 1 Thessalonians 2:13
- 2 Timothy 4:2
- 2 Peter 1:20–21

Scriptures for Further Meditation

- 1 Corinthians 3:5–17; 4:2; Ephesians 2:20; 2 Peter 1:3–4

Summary of Textbook Content

The foundation for **biblical missions** is the **authority** and **sufficiency of Scripture**. Scripture must permeate all aspects of the church's life through accurate gospel **proclamation** and ongoing teaching. However, current missiological thinking has expanded beyond the **Great Commission**, deprioritizing the Bible while adopting extrabiblical theories and practices. This is evident in certain **cultural accommodation** strategies that adapt the biblical and theological content of Scripture to the assumptions and values of the recipient **culture** in ways that compromise a biblical writer's intent for his text and its theology. Missions must return to Scripture's authority and sufficiency, remembering that the local church initiates missions, establishes new local churches, and holds missionaries accountable. Correcting flawed contemporary **missiology** requires recalibrating it according to the biblical view of the apostles.

Learning Objectives

- Understand the importance of biblical **inerrancy**, authority, sufficiency, and proper interpretive methods for missionaries to accurately convey the Word of God.
- Grasp the central role of the Bible in proclaiming the **gospel** and expressing theology.
- Recognize contemporary trends that have drifted from a biblical philosophy of missions.
- Identify various sources of authority in global contexts and how they have influenced receptivity to the authoritative written Word.

> The apostles were fixated on [God's Word]. For them, Scripture was critical in launching the church, crucial in the life of the church, and the core of their legacy for the church.
>
> **—Abner Chou, "Fidelity to the Word of God in Missions"**

Recall and Reflect

1. How does using the **grammatical-historical hermeneutic** help to prevent the **missionary** from falling into subjective, personal interpretation, or from forcing an illegitimate application for his hearers? [Chou, "Fidelity to the Word of God in Missions"]

2. Why is it important for missionaries to uphold the high view of Scripture held by the apostles? [Chou, "Fidelity to the Word of God in Missions"]

3. What are the practices that flow out of the central missionary activity of proclamation? Why are these practices important to accomplish on the mission field? [Burnett, "The Authority and the Sufficiency of the Bible for the Missionary Task"]

> The battle for missions in Africa is a battle over authority, over the Bible itself and for its accurate interpretation.
>
> **—Nathan Odede, "The Influence of African Authority Structures on Spirituality"**

4. What is meant by the term cultural accommodation? What is the difference between cultural accommodation and **linguistic accommodation**? Why is cultural accommodation dangerous for missions? [Burnett, "The Authority and the Sufficiency of the Bible for the Missionary Task"]

5. What is the source of the gospel proclaimer's authority? Why should this give them confidence in their missionary endeavors? [Burnett, "The Authority and the Sufficiency of the Bible for the Missionary Task"]

6. What are the three flaws that Christians must be careful to avoid in thinking about missionaries? [Doran, "A Biblical View of God's Servants, Work, and the Church"]

7. What is the standard by which Christ evaluates His servants? What are the implications for missions? [Doran, "A Biblical View of God's Servants, Work, and the Church"]

8. What is the relationship between God's "singular instrument" and the "singular reason" for missionaries to go to the **nations**? [Burnett, "The Authority and the Sufficiency of the Bible for the Missionary Task"]

9. What are the two poles of the spectrum of cross-cultural ministry along which missionaries operate? Which one is the biblical model, and why? [Burnett, "The Authority and the Sufficiency of the Bible for the Missionary Task"]

10. What are some sources of authority in African contexts that make **evangelism** more challenging? Be specific on how these sources minimize the recognition and worship of Christ. [Odede, "The Influence of African Authority Structures on Spirituality"]

Analyze

1. How might a missionary's view of biblical inerrancy affect their methodology of missions?

2. Should missionaries adjust their hermeneutic depending on their cultural context? Explain.

3. Why are the personal testimonies and personal opinions of missionaries insufficient for the gospel proclamation required in the Great Commission?

4. Is it the missionary's task to judge the significance that a biblical teaching has to the audience? Why or why not?

5. The world has witnessed more rapid change in the last century than perhaps ever before—technologically, economically, politically, and socially. What impact has this accelerated change had on missions? What advantages and disadvantages have arisen as a result?

6. It has been recognized that many Western missionaries are characterized by "hyper-individualism" and refuse to submit themselves to God-ordained authority. What are some specific problems that can result from this in their field service and in their relationship with their sending churches?

7. How does the Bible's claim to be "more sure" (2 Pet 1:19) shape and determine one's personal experience? How should this understanding affect one's approach to missions?

8. Explain the phrase "by one's own interpretation" in 2 Peter 1:20. What challenges arise when authority is tied to an individual and not to a written document?

9. Look at the bull's-eye chart in Figure 1 and do the following:
   a. Write out how your doctrine affects your priorities and your approaches to conducting at least two of the following ministries: evangelism, **discipleship**, **church planting**, vocational ministry.

Figure 1.1

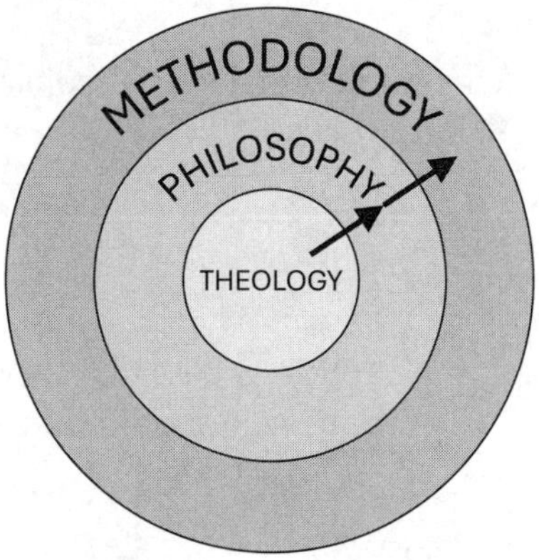

METHODOLOGY
PHILOSOPHY
THEOLOGY

b. Drawing from your own experience, describe how at least two theological convictions of your local church, training institution, or missions organization have led to specific ministry philosophies and actual methods for each.

Implement

1. How would you walk a new convert in a foreign field through the doctrine of biblical inerrancy? What Scriptures would you use? How would you explain the importance of this doctrine, especially if such a term and concept is foreign to him or her?

2. How might the missionary use Scripture to deal with those who view personal experiences and prophecies as authoritative?

3. Can you think of at least one way you might need to adjust your thinking to place what Scripture says above your own understanding or experience? What is a step you can make to change your thoughts in that area?

4. In what ways might your activities reveal that you have a love for human wisdom? How can you guard yourself against it? Be specific.

5. How have you seen the content of Scripture accommodated to local, contemporary ways of thinking in your context?

6. How might you be able to leverage global threats to missions as opportunities for the gospel?

7. Seeing how the **church** has endured dark chapters in the past and, in some places, the present (communism, fascism, terrorism, etc.), how are you thinking through current issues and the ways in which they might affect your local church?

Ask a Missionary

1. How do you model the sufficiency of Scripture in your missionary activities, whether proclamation or practical service? How do you guard yourself from looking outside the Bible to form your missionary practice?

2. What false religions or **worldviews** have a stronghold in your context, and what impact have they had on a person's ability to embrace the Word of God as authoritative and sufficient?

3. Have you seen culturally driven **hermeneutics** of Scripture employed in your context? How so? What are the implications?

4. What are the sources of ultimate authority in your context? How have you been able to use biblical truth to engage with different authority structures?

> Believers are commissioned by the Master to do the work He assigned, not to make up new plans or follow subjective dreams. Christians are commissioned servants, not entrepreneurs.
>
> **—David Doran, "A Biblical View of God's Servants, Work, and the Church"**

5. Have any recent local, national, or global developments complicated your missionary efforts? How have you handled such changes?

6. What unbiblical approaches to missions have you encountered, and how have you sought to maintain a biblically faithful approach?

Study the Scriptures

1. Study 2 Peter 1. How does this chapter correlate the doctrines of biblical inerrancy and sufficiency? What impact do these doctrines have on church leaders and church members specifically?

2. Read 2 Timothy and on a separate sheet of paper list each of Paul's instructions to Timothy. Count how many of these instructions pertain to God's Word. In the following space describe what impact these instructions have on a person's preparation for the mission field as well as their engagement while on the mission field.

3. Read Galatians 1–2. Paul mentions the gospel that the Galatian church received and also his own previous zeal for ancestral traditions. As well, he mentions that if anyone preaches a gospel different than the one the church had received, that person should be accursed. How do Paul's discussion points specifically apply to faith contexts that operate according to ancestral tradition and false gospels, such as many locations in Africa?

4. Study Psalm 119:89, 152; Isaiah 40:8; Matthew 24:35; and 1 Peter 1:23–25. What is the significance for your context and in your generation that Scripture is fixed in eternity past for an eternal future?

5. Draw up a list of general ministry principles that can be gleaned from 1 Corinthians 3:5–17. How might these principles help the missionary to avoid making the same mistakes that the Corinthians made?

6. Study 1 Thessalonians 2:4; Galatians 1:10; and 2 Corinthians 5:9. Whose approval should the missionary be seeking? How might this look practically on the mission field, especially with a missionary's layers of accountability and support in the local and sending churches and agency?

Missions Research

1. How might the "African hermeneutic" differ from the hermeneutical method of the apostles? Search for missiology journals and written works that define and even defend the African hermeneutic, also called the "Afrocentric (or Africentric) hermeneutic."

2. Select a country that is known for practicing animism and also has a strong presence of Roman Catholicism or Eastern Orthodoxy, such as in certain countries of West Africa or an Ibero-American country. Conduct the following tasks and report your findings:
   a. Survey the practices of animistic worship. Search for tribal ceremonies that appear to depict ancestral worship and animistic sacrifices there.

   b. Survey the practices associated with the veneration of Mary and patron saints. You might begin by searching online for websites or media of Roman Catholic churches in that context, particularly for expressions and demonstrations of celebrations and worship practices.

   c. List and explain the similarities and potential differences between the animistic and Catholic or Orthodox practices.

> When Scripture is made the authority, then the missionary has to develop a biblical philosophy of ministry consistent with the Scriptures. Then he will have a church that is able to fulfill the Great Commission, a church from which the word of Christ "sounds forth" into the world around it (1 Thess 1:8).
>
> **—Mark Tatlock, "Missiological Application: God-Ordained Authority in Missions"**

3. Research the World Missionary Conference in Edinburgh in 1910 in original documents and reports from the time, as well as from treatments by missions historians. What was the impact of this conference on the ecumenical dialogue between evangelicals and Roman Catholics? What theological implications came from this conference? What reporting differences do you notice between, on the one hand, ecumenical Protestants and Roman Catholics and, on the other hand, conservative evangelicals?

4. Research the 2010 Cape Town Commitment (CTC) document, which reflects the proceedings of the Third Lausanne Congress on World Evangelization. Record how the "gospel" and "the work of the gospel" are defined and described. List which expressions seem to match the biblical standard of gospel ministry and which seem to differ. In what ways might the expressions embolden or deter the missionary from the primary task of gospel proclamation?

Application Projects

1. On a separate sheet of paper, construct a personal doctrinal statement on biblical **inspiration**, inerrancy, authority, and sufficiency, which you could hand to a potential supporting church or **missions agency**. Be specific and make use of the relevant biblical passages. This may be done individually but doing it with a team is preferable.

2. The unbelieving world sources their ultimate authority in people, positions, symbols, structures, or concepts other than the Bible. Research three target audiences in different locations, and determine their primary source(s) of authority. For each authority identified, write a response identifying how a missionary or pastor should correct the claim to authority with the biblical worldview.

Target Audience	Source of Authority	Biblical Correction

3. If you are preparing for missionary work or helping someone to prepare, work to answer this question: "How will you safeguard your commitment to the authority and sufficiency of Scripture amid the cultural pressures you will face in your field context that may call that commitment into question? What safeguards or accountability measures will you put in place?" In the following table, list potential cultural pressures that may undermine biblical authority. Then in the right column, detail accountability measures and safeguards you will put in place when each pressure arises in your life and ministry.

Cultural Pressures	Safeguards

4. Missionaries can drift from biblical missions while doing many seemingly beneficial things. Answer these questions as a leader (actual or potential), who has encountered missionaries who have drifted from faithfully preaching the biblical gospel in some way.

a. List ways that missionary unfaithfulness can be seen in your context.

b. Describe how, as a leader, you will graciously but firmly call the unfaithful missionary back to scriptural fidelity.

c. What processes and structures can be put in place to prevent such drift in the future?

Come and See

Missions in the Old Testament

Textbook Content

CHAPTER 4: The Old Testament: God's Heart for the World, by Michael A. Grisanti

> **INSERT 4.1:** Does the Old Testament Have a Great Commission? by Kyle C. Dunham

CHAPTER 5: One Holy Race: Ethnicity and the People of God, by Scott Callaham

Key Memory Verse

And Yahweh said to Abram, "Go forth from your land, and from your kin and from your father's house, to the land which I will show you; and I will make you a great nation, and I will bless you, and make your name great; and so you shall be a blessing; and I will bless those who bless you, and the one who curses you I will curse. And in you all the families of the earth will be blessed."

—GENESIS 12:1–3

Additional Memory Verses

- Genesis 1:26–27
- Genesis 3:15
- Exodus 19:5–6
- Isaiah 42:1–9
- Isaiah 49:6

Scriptures for Further Meditation

- Deuteronomy 26:16–19; 1 Samuel 16:7; Isaiah 43:10–12; 45:20–25; Acts 1:8; 13:47; Ephesians 2:14–18; Revelation 7:9–10

Summary of Textbook Content

The Old Testament proclaims God's missionary heart for the world. Though the Great Commission was not provided until the New Testament, the Old Testament lays the foundation for God's redemptive plan. In turn, the New Testament consists of an amplification of the Old Testament promise that the nations will experience God's salvation. Moreover, the topic of missions in the Old Testament is characterized primarily by an inward trajectory ("come and see"), which then transitions in the New Testament to an outward trajectory ("go and make"). The goal of God's redemptive plan has always been to create "one holy race" that consists of a unified group from every nation, tribe, and tongue who will worship Christ for all eternity.

Learning Objectives

- Understand God's heart for the world.
- Understand how the Old Testament relates to the Great Commission.
- Understand Israel's role in God's plan of redemption.
- Identify key biblical passages that reveal the character of God and the witnessing activities of His people in the Old Testament.
- Understand the meaning and significance of "ethnicity."
- Recognize that the church is "one holy race" consisting of disciples from all the nations of the world.

> God's blessing through Abraham to the nations has been set in motion by Christ, and the Church must take up the task with urgency and faithfulness.
>
> **—Kyle Dunham, "Does the Old Testament Have a Great Commission?"**

Recall and Reflect

1. When did God first reveal His intention to rule throughout the earth? [Grisanti, "The Old Testament"]

2. Does the Old Testament have a Great Commission? In what ways does the Old Testament lay the theological groundwork for missions? Explain. [Grisanti, "Old Testament"; Dunham, "Does the Old Testament Have a Great Commission?"]

3. What differences in mission focus are there between Old Testament Israel and the church? [Grisanti, "Old Testament"; Dunham, "Does the Old Testament Have a Great Commission?"]

4. Describe Israel's role as a "special mediator" to the nations. [Grisanti, "The Old Testament"; Dunham, "Does the Old Testament Have a Great Commission?"]

5. How would you explain the difference between the terms "**centrifugal**" and "**centripetal**"? [Grisanti, "The Old Testament"; Dunham, "Does the Old Testament Have a Great Commission?"]

6. How do the authors support the argument from Scripture that Old Testament Israel is not a missionary nation? [Grisanti, "The Old Testament"; Dunham, "Does the Old Testament Have a Great Commission?"]

7. What is the biblical understanding of "race" and "ethnicity"? [Callaham, "One Holy Race"]

8. What is God's reason for introducing ethnic groups and nations into redemptive history? [Callaham, "Ony Holy Race"]

9. If biological heredity was not primary in setting Abraham and his descendants apart as the people of God, what was? How is this significant for those who were outside of the Hebrew ethnic group? [Callaham, "One Holy Race"]

10. What was the sin of the Judaizers in the early church? Why was it so harmful? [Callaham, "One Holy Race"]

Analyze

1. How does one's **anthropology** (the doctrine of man) influence one's view of ethnicity?

2. How does the Bible depict the nature of humanity with respect to ethnicity? What passages would you use to support the argument that there is "one holy race"?

3. What is always the basis of God's election?

4. The Judaizers promoted circumcision as a necessary mark of salvation. In what ways do you see people leaning on a personal quality or characteristic to find assurance of salvation or a sense of spiritual significance? How might you encounter this in your missionary work?

5. How would you present Israel's role in God's worldwide plan to an unbeliever? How about in a context that is unfavorable toward the Jewish people today?

6. What is the relationship between Israel and Yahweh's judgment in the Old Testament? How does this awareness influence one's attitude toward other nations and toward missions in general?

7. What impact should God's intentions to bless the world through Israel have on your missiology?

Implement

1. What does it mean to be a "witness" for God? How is this witness modeled in your life? How can you grow in it? Be specific. See Isaiah 43:10–12; Luke 24:48; Acts 1:8.

2. How can you implement a biblical understanding of race and ethnicity in your evangelism and outreach in your local cross-cultural context? Be specific.

3. How could a biblical understanding of God's purposes for Israel aid you in apologetics and evangelism to Jewish people?

4. How can you use the Old Testament, through the ministry of preaching and teaching, to educate and energize missions within your local church? What are the most relevant passages?

5. How does an understanding of God's worldwide plan of salvation from the Old Testament influence how you read the Bible?

6. As a missionary, how might you go about teaching a new **people group** about the relationship between God's judgment and Israel's future repentance?

Ask a Missionary

1. How has your study of the Old Testament shaped your understanding of missions?

> The unity of "every nation and all tribes and peoples and tongues" (Rev 7:9) in heaven is due to the atoning work of Christ to redeem the elect of every ethnicity for the sake of the worship of Christ forever.
>
> **—Scott Callaham, "One Holy Race: Ethnicity and the People of God"**

2. What impact has teaching/preaching the Old Testament had on those you minister to?

3. Have you encountered ethnic tensions in your missionary work? If so, how have you used the truth of God's Word to overcome those tensions?

4. How have you seen Christ unite people with diverse backgrounds and interests? How do you ensure that your ministry efforts foster unity among various people?

Study the Scriptures

1. What is the significance of Genesis 3:15 as it relates to God's redemptive plan?

2. In a bulleted list on a separate sheet of paper, catalog God's redemptive plan chronologically through the book of Genesis, citing the most relevant passages. Look especially for the keyword *seed* or *descendant(s)* and for other repeated themes as they are progressively developed through the book. Describe how these passages and themes display God's heart for the world.

3. Trace the concept of nations, ethnicities, and languages in Genesis 10–11, citing verses, and show how these distinctions inform an understanding of God's choosing of and purposes for Abraham in Genesis 12:1–3.

4. What are the theological implications of 1 Samuel 16:7? What are the missiological implications?

5. Locate on the contemporary world map in Figure 2.1 the countries of origin or countries of residence other than Israel for these six Old Testament figures: Moses, Ruth, Elijah, Elisha, Daniel, and Jonah. Can you identify the countries of at least five more figures? Use a Bible atlas to help, recognizing that some place names and inhabiting peoples have changed since Bible times.

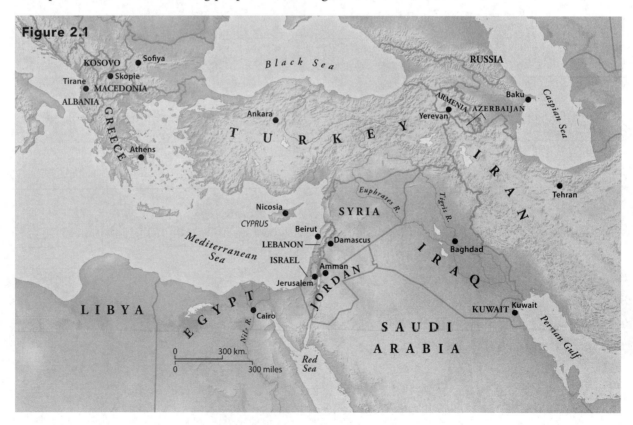

Figure 2.1

6. Study Isaiah 45:20–25. What is the basis for God's appeal for people of all nations to turn to Him and be saved?

> The Bible is permeated from beginning to end with God's own great mission—
> "Salvation belongs to our God" (Rev 7:10). He will bring His sovereign and redemptive
> intentions to pass. Whatever Old Testament believers did to put God's character
> on display and whatever New Testament Christ followers do as the outflow of
> their salvation represents the participation of God's people in His mission.
> —**Michael A. Grisanti, "The Old Testament: God's Heart for the World"**

Missions Research

1. Compare and contrast Islam among "Abrahamic religions," and explain how Christians should respond to the assertion that Muslims have a mutual basis of faith. How does Islam depart from biblical Christianity?

2. Research how faithful missionaries from the eighteenth to twentieth centuries used the term *heathen* when referring to the people to which they were sent. Choose a few missionaries and complete the following prompts:
   a. Describe how they use the term *heathen* in relation to the people's local beliefs and practices. Cite some uses of the term in their writings and provide context for understanding their use of the term.

   b. List and define three to five titles that have replaced *heathen* in the common parlance of the contemporary church.

   c. How do missionaries reference the people they serve on the mission field? Do they use any of the historic or contemporary titles today?

Application Projects

1. Based on the textbook material, use the Venn diagram in Figure 2.2 to compare and contrast God's purposes and strategies as revealed in the Old and New Testaments. Make note of the differences and similarities. Write a brief explanation of your findings with the intention of creating a presentation to a group, such as a Bible study or class.

Figure 2.2   God's Purposes & Strategies

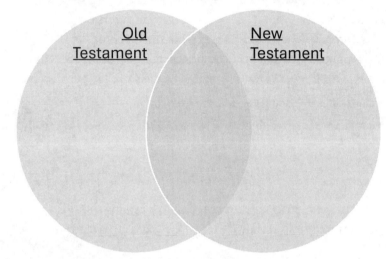

2. Consider the diagram in Figure 2.3 comparing the **witness** strategies of Old Testament Israel with that of the church according to the centripetal and centrifugal principles. Then answer these questions:

Figure 2.3

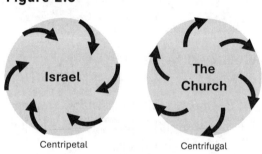

a. What might be some centripetal activities of missionaries and local church leaders today?

b. What are some Old Testament witnessing strategies that you identify as useful to your engagement with international unbelievers living near you? Explain how you might employ those strategies practically in your daily life as a means of accomplishing the Great Commission.

3. Local churches can sometimes get caught up in subtle forms of ethnic favoritism, which Callaham calls "skin-color-conscious religion." How would you as a church leader (actual or hypothetical) correct believers, including fellow leaders, who have fallen into this sin? In the space provided identify a range of problems related to ethnocentrism (actual or hypothetical). Then on a separate sheet of paper outline in a flowchart a multistep process for addressing and correcting one of those problems, starting with your observation of the problem, your active approach to correct it, and activities that the church can undertake to demonstrate their restoration to unity.

LESSON 3

Go and Make

Missions in the New Testament

Textbook Content

CHAPTER 6: A Messiah for All Peoples: Christ's Affirmation of a Nonexclusive Gospel, by Mark Tatlock

CHAPTER 7: God's Invincible Plan: A Structural Study of Acts, by Alejandro Peluffo

> **INSERT 7.1:** Practical Pauline Missions: Paul's Missions to Pisidian Antioch and Philippi, by William D. Barrick

CHAPTER 8: The Kingdom of God in the Church Age, by Chris Burnett

Key Memory Verse

For I am not ashamed of the gospel, for it is the power of God for salvation to everyone who believes, to the Jew first and also to the Greek.

—ROMANS 1:16

Additional Memory Verses

- Luke 24:46–47
- Acts 1:8
- Acts 2:38–39
- Acts 6:7
- 2 Timothy 2:8–9

Scriptures for Further Meditation

- Genesis 1:26–28; 12:1–3; Isaiah 49:6; Acts 13:46–47; 2 Peter 3:9

Summary of Textbook Content

God's kingdom plan of salvation encompasses people from all nations, with Christ's messianic ministry fulfilling the prophetic vision of this outcome. The book of Acts traces how the early church continued Christ's ministry as the gospel spread geographically and cross-culturally according to God's sovereign plan. Paul's adaptable missionary methods further communicate the unchanging message of the gospel and the nature of God's kingdom in the Church age. A biblical understanding of God's kingdom should shape the missionary's priorities and perspective, keeping in mind that the church proclaims the gospel to bring people into God's kingdom but does not build the kingdom itself.

Learning Objectives

- Understand the biblical basis for the universal scope of the gospel.
- Grasp the centrality of the **kingdom of God** theme in Scripture.
- Identify the relationship between the church and the kingdom of God.
- Understand the structure and themes of the book of Acts in light of God's plan to spread the gospel cross-culturally.
- Comprehend Paul's missionary journeys as models of adaptive methods united around an unchanging message.
- Grasp how a biblically accurate theology of God's kingdom should shape missionary priorities and perspectives.

> Jesus' gospel, though coming through God's chosen nation Israel, is nonexclusive; it is for all peoples. . . . Men and women from every nation are included in redemption's scope.
>
> **—Mark Tatlock, "A Messiah for All Peoples: Christ's Affirmation of a Nonexclusive Gospel"**

Recall and Reflect

1. Why, in contradiction to biblical prophecy, did postexilic Israel develop a view of God's redemptive plan that excluded Gentiles? What impact did this have on their expectations of the coming Messiah? [Tatlock, "A Messiah for All Peoples"]

2. What is the first reference in the New Testament to the inclusive scope of Jesus' messiahship? What is so significant about that reference? [Tatlock, "A Messiah for All Peoples"]

3. What was it that caused the people of Nazareth to so quickly change from anticipation of Jesus as the Messiah to animosity and hatred of Him? [Tatlock, "A Messiah for All Peoples"]

4. What was significant about the area of the temple that Jesus cleansed? What did Jesus communicate through His act of cleansing the temple? [Tatlock, "A Messiah for All Peoples"]

5. What are the theme, purpose, and major divisions of the book of Acts? [Peluffo, "God's Invincible Plan"]

6. What was Paul's motive for missions? Who was Paul's target audience? [Barrick, "Practical Pauline Missions"]

7. How else do Peluffo and Barrick explain Paul as a model of a faithful Christian witness? [Peluffo, "God's Invincible Plan"; Barrick, "Practical Pauline Missions"]

8. What is the earliest statement regarding man's role in God's kingdom plan? [Burnett, "The Kingdom of God in the Church Age"]

9. What are some contemporary mistaken ideas of the church's relationship to the kingdom of God? [Burnett, "The Kingdom of God in the Church Age"]

Analyze

1. Why do you think Jesus was so vocal about affirming the faith of Gentile believers throughout His ministry?

2. Why is it important to remember that the book of Acts is usually descriptive and not prescriptive of missions work?

3. In view of God's sovereign plan in the book of Acts, what role does God's sovereignty play in missions today?

4. What effect did persecution have on the early church? What implications does this carry for the church today?

5. Why might it be a problem to see the theme of missions in every passage of the Bible? In other words, what is wrong with the **missional hermeneutic**?

6. How does the coming reality of the Millennium affect a missionary's ethics and philosophy of mercy ministries today?

7. Explain the difference between societal transformation as the missionary's objective versus a possible soteriological by-product. Why is this difference significant?

> In view of the biblical understanding of the kingdom, the task of the missionary is to proclaim repentance to the nations because the King is coming and today He offers kingdom citizenship to all who will believe in Him.
>
> **—Chris Burnett, "The Kingdom of God in the Church Age"**

Implement

1. How can churches today practice biblical inclusivity? How does it differ from modern-day notions of tolerance and inclusiveness?

2. How can Peluffo's observations of the structure and purpose of Acts be incorporated into a church's philosophy of ministry? Consider discussing the philosophy of ministry at your local church with a pastor/elder as it relates to the book of Acts.

3. In what ways do you need to become more selfless in your evangelistic efforts like the apostle Paul, who though he was "free from all" made himself a "slave to all" that he might win more to Christ (1 Cor 9:19)?

4. How does the book of Acts help set expectations and prepare you for dealing with opposition and suffering in ministry? How are you presently preparing yourself to face the same threats?

5. How would you respond to someone who says that the kingdom of God is a present visible reality? What is your preferred way of describing the kingdom of God?

Ask a Missionary

1. What impact have Christ's interactions with Gentiles in the Gospels had on your work as a missionary?

2. How have you attempted to facilitate a church environment that is welcoming to people from different backgrounds?

3. How has the book of Acts shaped your view on missions?

4. How has your understanding of Christ's coming kingdom affected how you approach missions?

Study the Scriptures

1. Read the story of the good Samaritan in Luke 10:25–37. What does the parable teach that is instructive for the church regarding cross-cultural relationships?

> Let Jesus' witnesses . . . follow the early church's example and finish their stories likewise: "preaching the kingdom of God and teaching concerning the Lord Jesus Christ with all confidence, unhindered" (Acts 28:31). Indeed, may God grant it to be so.
>
> —Alejandro Peluffo, "God's Invincible Plan: A Structural Study of Acts"

2. Study Isaiah 19:16–25. Discuss Israel's role in the future *eschaton* and explain these implications for missions today.

3. How does Galatians 3:1–14 relate to the blessing and faith motifs of Genesis 12:1–3 and 15:6? Why does this matter for missions?

4. How does the Hebrews 11 "Hall of Faith" describe its members? What is the ultimate result of their faith? Who from the list are Gentiles, and how does their faith relate to Genesis 12:1–3?

5. Use the map in Figure 3.1 to chart the routes of Paul's three missionary journeys in Acts 13:4–14:8; 15:36–18:22; and 18:23–21:16, respectively. Use a different colored pen or pencil for each journey. Connect the cities in his travels by drawing arrows, and indicate where he planted churches or made disciples by drawing stars. Use a Bible atlas or study Bible to help you, but read the text of Acts. It might be helpful to label each location with the corresponding chapter and verse reference(s) in which it is found. Note that many routes and cities will be used more than once.

Missions Research

1. Using a Bible dictionary, the map in Figure 3.1, and the following table, write in the present-day city names that are equivalent to the first-century cities—or, if the latter are no longer inhabited, then present-day cities nearby them—that either Paul visited or are locations of believers referenced in Acts. Choose three of the cities (not regions) in the list to research further, and if possible, find a faithful gospel-witnessing church that is still standing in that city. Provide some basic information about it. If you cannot find a faithful church, describe what false religions or worldviews predominate the city instead.

First-Century City/Region	Present-Day City/Region	Present-Day Gospel-Witnessing Church (or Explanation If Lacking)
Iconium	Konya, Turkey	
Asia		
Ephesus		
Troas		
Berea		
Macedonia		
Philippi		
Thessalonica		
Corinth		
Phoenicia		

Figure 3.1

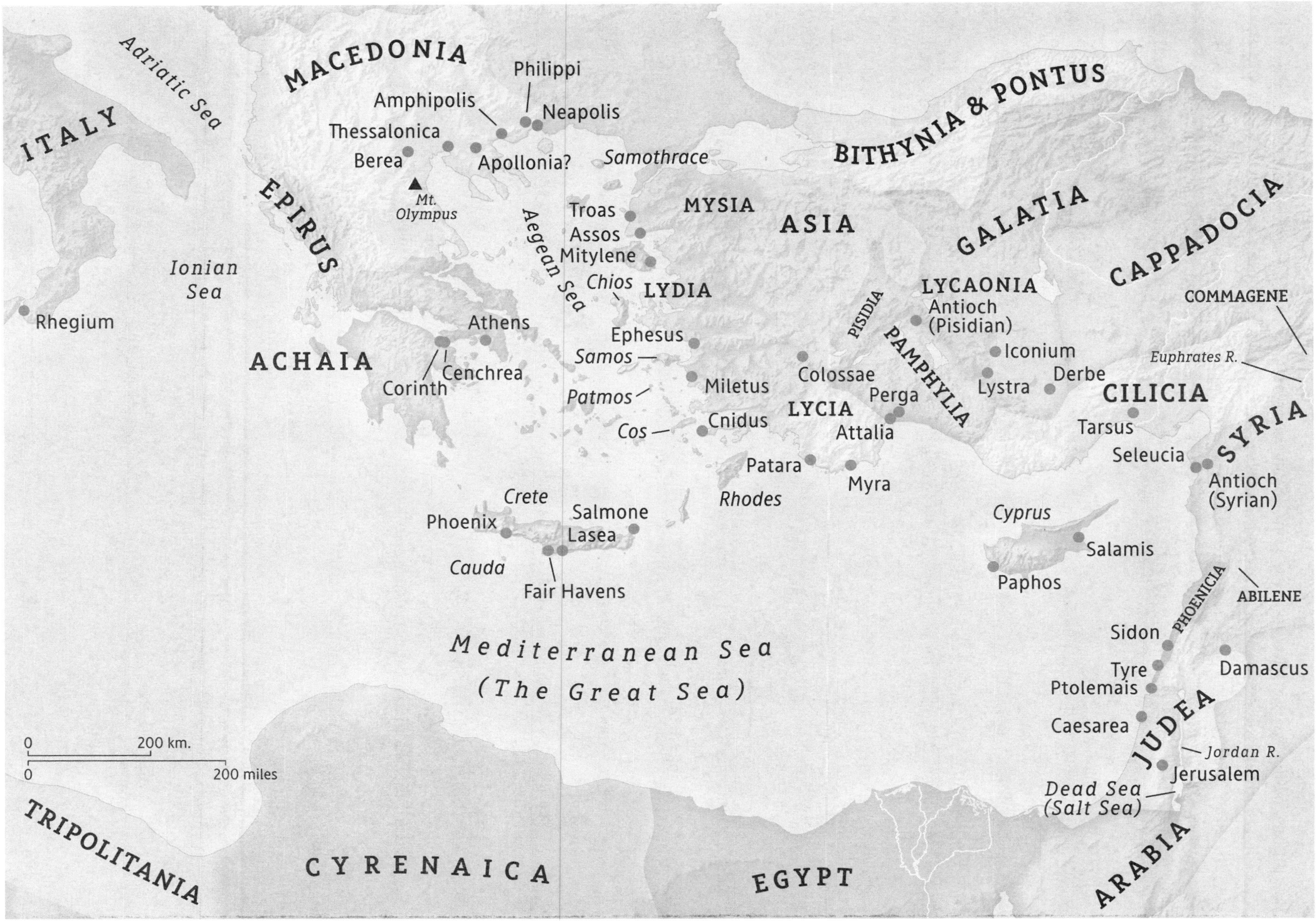

ITALY
Adriatic Sea
MACEDONIA
Philippi
Amphipolis
Neapolis
Thessalonica
Berea
Apollonia?
Samothrace
BITHYNIA & PONTUS
EPIRUS
Mt. Olympus
Troas
Assos
Mitylene
MYSIA
ASIA
GALATIA
CAPPADOCIA
Aegean Sea
Ionian Sea
Chios
LYDIA
LYCAONIA
Antioch (Pisidian)
COMMAGENE
Rhegium
Athens
Ephesus
PISIDIA
PAMPHYLIA
Iconium
Euphrates R.
ACHAIA
Samos
Colossae
Lystra
Derbe
Corinth
Cenchrea
Miletus
Perga
CILICIA
Patmos
LYCIA
Cos
Cnidus
Attalia
Tarsus
SYRIA
Seleucia
Patara
Myra
Antioch (Syrian)
Crete
Rhodes
Salmone
Cyprus
Phoenix
Lasea
Salamis
Cauda
Fair Havens
Paphos
PHOENICIA
ABILENE
Sidon
Mediterranean Sea
(The Great Sea)
Damascus
Tyre
Ptolemais
JUDEA
Caesarea
Jordan R.
0
200 km.
0
200 miles
Jerusalem
Dead Sea (Salt Sea)
TRIPOLITANIA
CYRENAICA
EGYPT
ARABIA

2. Some theological systems argue for a one-to-one continuity between the creation mandate and the Great Commission. How might using missionaries to bring a "sociopolitical manifestation of the kingdom of God" be a less-than-faithful approach to missions? To answer this question, research sociopolitical engagement approaches in a specific global context, such as those occurring in a nation (e.g., El Salvador; Nagaland, India) or in a society (e.g., university outreach in Nairobi, Kenya; border towns of Texas, USA).

3. Research the "missional hermeneutic" and the grammatical-historical hermeneutic. Explain at least five potential missiological drawbacks of using the missional hermeneutic compared to the literal grammatical-historical hermeneutic in one specific mission field context of your choosing, such as a nation or a particular city or society within a specific city (e.g., the rural villages of Luwero, Uganda; the Brahmin population of West Mumbai).

4. God's ambassadors always suffer some form of opposition to the gospel, ranging from minor inconveniences to martyrdom. Research some reports of the treatment of missionaries or local churches or believers in a location known for persecuting those who proclaim the gospel. Then on a separate sheet of paper do the following:
   a. Divide the sheet into three columns. In the first column, list specific ways these believers have suffered at the hands of their government, citizens, families, and friends.
   b. Then review the book of Acts for references to the suffering for the gospel that the earliest missionaries, church leaders, and believers experienced. Match up the similar experiences of opposition or persecution between the contemporary and the ancient believers by listing the latter in the second column.
   c. Finally, adjacent to each match-up in the second column, write a brief statement in the third column articulating the similarities.

Application Projects

1. On a separate sheet of paper, create a chart of key passages from both the Old and New Testaments demonstrating the progressive **revelation** of God's redemptive plan for the Gentiles. Many of the passages are referenced in the textbook chapters 4–8. Determine a teaching outline based on your preferred structure: chronological history, canonical order, biblical genre, and so on. Turn it into a message that you could use in a Sunday school class or for a small group Bible study, if granted the opportunity by your local church leaders.

2. Create a presentation on the book of Acts with the goal of presenting it to the missions committee or elders at your church. Incorporate the following items in the presentation:
   a. An outline of the book along with key passages in each chapter.
   b. Passages that deal with these key ideas: preaching and teaching; the Word of God; conversion and discipleship; persecution and suffering.
   c. A survey of God's attributes (perfections) that are on display throughout the book, with verse references.
   d. Key takeaways related to how Acts informs and applies to the local church and mission field today.

3. Consider the elder board at a sending church. If the elders discover that one of their missionaries is in some way distorting the gospel by practicing an unbiblical kingdom theology, how should they intervene? Create a flowchart that moves from a list of observable problems that typically result from such kingdom theology, followed by steps needed to resolve each perceived problem. Make sure to identify strategies for investigating your concerns, then for gently confronting the issues, then for restoring the missionary to or, if necessary, removing the missionary from ministry. Note that flowcharts—step-by-step pathways with arrows—also show alternate paths based on decision points in the process, which in this case would depend on the elder board's resolution process and the missionary's response. Along the steps of your flowchart, cite the biblical rationale for your actions.

Hearers of the Word

Understanding Christ's Mandate in the Great Commission

Textbook Content

CHAPTER 9: The Composite Teaching of the Great Commission Passages, by Chris Burnett

    INSERT 9.1: Examples of Less-Than-Great Commissions in Latin America, by Josué Pineda Dale

CHAPTER 10: Make Disciples: What the Great Commission Means and What We Must Do, by Scott Callaham

    INSERT 10.1: Essentials to Discipleship Strategies, by Phillip F. Foley

CHAPTER 11: The Message of Our Mission, by Michael Riccardi

    INSERT 11.1: The Missionary Must Call for Repentance, by Bill Shannon

    INSERT 11.2: Decisions and Discipleship: The Relationship between Conversion and Obedience, by Rodney Andersen

    INSERT 11.3: The Commercialization of Christianity in South Africa, by Nathan Odede

Key Memory Verse

And Jesus came up and spoke to them, saying, "All authority has been given to Me in heaven and on earth. Go therefore and make disciples of all the nations, baptizing them in the name of the Father and the Son and the Holy Spirit, teaching them to keep all that I commanded you; and behold, I am with you always, even to the end of the age."

—MATTHEW 28:18–20

Additional Memory Verses

- Matthew 9:37–38
- Mark 16:15–16

- Luke 24:46–49
- John 20:21–23
- Acts 1:8
- 2 Corinthians 5:18–21

Scriptures for Further Meditation

- Matthew 13:1–9; Mark 6:12; Luke 5:31–32; John 14:6; Romans 3:23; 6:23; 10:17; 1 Corinthians 15:3–4

Summary of Textbook Content

The Great Commission is Christ's global mandate for missions. That mandate, which He left for His disciples, is the same mandate that missionaries must follow today. Sending out missionaries to preach and teach the gospel to all the nations of the earth is the heart of the Great Commission. While it has been passed down in Holy Scripture, many groups have fallen short of the biblical standard by adding to the gospel with "less-than-great commissions." However, missionaries are deemed effective and faithful only insofar as they preach biblical repentance and engage in biblical discipleship. True conversion will be apparent over time as professing believers demonstrate good works that reveal the evidence of saving faith. Missionaries toil and strive in support of this divine work.

Learning Objectives

- Be able to biblically explain the mission of the church and the Great Commission.
- Articulate an accurate gospel message.
- Grasp the discipleship process.
- Recognize biblical repentance and how it manifests in a believer's life.
- Recognize the difference between conversion and obedience.
- Understand the role of baptism in biblical discipleship.
- Discern the measure of true success within missions.

Recall and Reflect

1. What does Christ supply and promise to His disciples in the Great Commission? [Burnett, "The Composite Teaching of the Great Commission Passages"]

2. What are the three core actions of making disciples as revealed in the Great Commission? [Burnett, "The Composite Teaching of the Great Commission Passages"; Callaham, "Make Disciples"]

3. What are the three "less-than-great" commissions identified in Latin America and their core theological beliefs? [Pineda Dale, "Examples of Less-Than-Great Commissions"]

4. What is the reason for seeing the Great Commission as "the" mission of the church? [Callaham, "Make Disciples"]

5. What does Riccardi say is "the great business of the church's mission"? What four components must be included in the message of the mission? [Riccardi, "The Message of Our Mission"]

6. What is the biblical definition of repentance? How does biblical repentance manifest in the life of a believer? [Shannon, "The Missionary Must Call for Repentance"]

7. What are the consequences of missionaries pursuing "decisions for Christ"? [Andersen, "Decisions and Discipleship"]

8. If God does not judge a missionary's life by the number of conversions in his or her ministry, what does God judge a missionary's life by? [Andersen, "Decisions and Discipleship"]

9. What solution is recommended concerning the problems of charismatic and **syncretistic** churches in South Africa? [Odede, "The Commercialization of Christianity in South Africa"]

Analyze

1. What is the difference between evangelism and discipleship? How does missionary work relate to both?

2. What is the aim of discipleship? Are there such things as context-specific discipleship? How do you differentiate between the essential components of discipleship and those that are context-specific?

3. How does a biblical understanding of baptism inform the disciple-making process? Why is it important to derive one's theology of baptism from the Bible alone?

One who departs from God's Word is bound to fail. This is a general principle in theology and in life, but the same applies to missions.

—Josué Pineda Dale

4. Compare and contrast the five Great Commission passages. In the table provided on page 000, identify textual and conceptual parallels and distinctions. (See the examples given in the first and last rows.) Use an additional sheet if needed.

Key Terms/ Concepts	Matt 28:18–20	Mark 16:15–20	Luke 24:46–49	John 20:21–23	Acts 1:8
Forgiveness	—	—	"repentance for forgiveness of sins" (v. 47)	"If you forgive the sins of any" (v. 23)	—
Unique Terms/ Concepts		"signs" (vv. 17, 20) "drink any deadly poison" (v. 18)			

5. What "less-than-great" commissions are promoted in your own context? In what ways do they deviate from the biblical mandate?

6. Why does defining discipleship as "whatever a missionary does in contact with host nation people" fall short of the biblical standard of going, baptizing, and teaching?

7. How does one's understanding of the sinfulness of man affect one's approach to evangelism?

Implement

1. How often do you think about the command to "make disciples"? In what ways can you grow in obedience to this command?

2. Are you showing partiality in whom you evangelize? How can you grow in your willingness to preach the gospel to every person?

3. What are your thoughts on more informal forms of discipling? If you are accustomed to informal forms, what do you think about more formal, study-based forms? Can you think of times when both methods can be helpful?

4. Say there is a new convert in your local congregation. However, they tell you that they want to wait on being baptized even though they understand the meaning of baptism. How would you respond to this believer?

5. What would be your response if donors are expecting decisions for Christ? Would you allow that to drive your approach toward missions? If not, why not?

6. How should a biblical understanding of faith and obedience guide your discipling efforts?

7. Consider carefully your own church's outreach efforts. How is your church doing? How could you possibly encourage growth in its execution of the Great Commission?

Ask a Missionary

1. What are your priorities in ministry, evangelism, and discipleship in your context? How do these manifest practically? Are there external restrictions you must deal with?

> God will not judge a missionary's life by his number of conversions, but by faithfulness in life and teaching. Let missionaries then watch closely their doctrines of faith and obedience, and so be found as good and faithful servants.
>
> **—Rodney Andersen, "Decisions and Discipleship: The Relationship between Conversion and Obedience"**

2. What passages of Scripture have had the greatest influence on you as they relate to evangelism and discipleship?

3. In your missionary work, how do you look for fruit, call for fruit, and cultivate fruit in your life and in the lives of those to whom you are ministering?

4. Please explain what baptism looks like in your context. How soon are new believers baptized? How do you prepare them for baptism? Where are the baptisms performed? What are the most common misunderstandings you encounter regarding baptism?

5. What false or compromised versions of the Great Commission, in your opinion, are you encountering on the mission field? Have such viewpoints and practices had an impact on your ministry directly or indirectly? How have you sought to address them in your teaching and activities?

Study the Scriptures

1. Read Matthew 13:1–23. What do the different soils represent? Which soil represents true saving faith? How do you know? Inform your answers with Jesus' previous teaching in Matthew 7:21–29.

2. Study John 20:23. Burnett argued from this text that the messenger of God is called to carry out both forgiveness and judgment "in new global contexts." Explain each of these terms and their significance in John 20:23.

3. Study John 14:6. Christ refers to Himself as the Way, the Truth, and the Life. How might these titles and the exclusivity of Christ impact discipleship in regions where religious pluralism, relativism, syncretism, and/or inclusivism compete as ideologies and worldviews in opposition to Christianity?

4. Read Romans 1–8 and trace Paul's gospel presentation. What does Paul emphasize? What distinctives of the gospel are found in this section of Scripture?

Missions Research

1. Study baptism in the New Testament using a concordance or Bible software to find occurrences of the terms *baptism* and *baptize*. Consider the constraints that believer's full-immersion water baptism in the book of Acts places on the practice of baptism today. Do the following tasks:
   a. Identify contexts in which the practice of the believer's full-immersion water baptism is either unknown, resisted, or adapted into some other form, and provide any pertinent information you find (e.g., some "Hindu Christ followers" are encouraged by missionaries to replace the practice of water baptism with a puja ceremony; one missionary in Chad has to bring in water by sacks on donkeys and so struggles to collect enough for full-immersion baptism).

   b. On a separate sheet of paper, write out a biblical defense of believer's baptism for disciples in any context, which includes a response to one actual case where the practice is resisted or modified in a church plant or church-planting movement.

2. Research field reports of big numbers of daily conversions through missionaries and church leaders by doing the following:
   a. Find one report for each of the following global regions: North America, Ibero-America, Europe, Africa, Asia Pacific, Middle East and North Africa (MENA). Draw from missionary newsletters, web pages, or missiological journals and magazines (many of which are freely accessible online).
   b. Assess the reports based on the biblical principles of the gospel and the Great Commission that you have studied in this section of the textbook. Describe your findings below.

3. Draft a comparison chart of key elements of the biblical gospel to the corresponding ideas within at least two of the following world religions and/or worldviews: Roman Catholicism, Eastern Orthodoxy, Hinduism, Islam, Buddhism, African traditional religions, animism, **liberation theology**, secular humanism.

Theme	Biblical Gospel Truths with Verses	Selection 1: _____	Selection 2: _____
God/Deity			
Jesus Christ/Revealer			
Man			
Sin			
Redemption			

The goal of being sent as an ambassador of Christ to the nations need not change for one who goes less distance than another, as long as the goal remains to see the gospel extend out in concentric rings to and through the hearer from "the nations."

—Chris Burnett, "The Composite Teaching of the Great Commission Passages"

Application Projects

1. Find someone who has expressed interest in being discipled. Using the following question checklist, spend some time with the person, ask the following questions, record your experience, and in a separate document create a discipleship plan for them. Before meeting with this person for the first time, present your plan to an elder of your local church and receive his feedback.

SPIRITUAL QUESTIONS TO ASK THEM:

- What is your testimony?
- What are your spiritual disciplines?
- What struggles with sin are you comfortable sharing with me today?
- How do you think the Lord has gifted you?
- Where are you presently serving?
- What are your ministry aspirations?

- How can I help facilitate sanctification in your life?
- How can I be praying for you?
- How are your current life circumstances influencing the way you view God and His character?

LOGISTICAL QUESTIONS TO ASK THEM:

- Where can we meet?

- When/how often can we meet?

DISCIPLESHIP PLAN TO DEVELOP AFTERWARD:

- What sin issues were identified?
- What biblical passages address these?
- What resources can be provided or recommended?

- What area(s) will you encourage the brother or sister to serve in?

2. Missionaries may never see a conversion to Christ during their entire time on the mission field. Write a letter to a missionary that your church supports, and encourage them in their labor for the Lord. Reference Bible passages that encourage with the sovereignty of God in salvation and the measure of faithfulness as a steward of the gospel.

3. Create a bulleted list of four biblical terms that you frequently use when you present the gospel. Write out a definition for each term that someone with no preexisting knowledge of the Bible could understand. Use resources like a concordance or an expository dictionary to help you survey the biblical usage of the terms. Then note biblical passages that help capture the terms' meanings, and add some of your own illustrations to help illuminate the biblical concepts they convey.

Doers of the Word

Obeying Christ's Mandate through Gospel Proclamation

Textbook Content

CHAPTER 12: One Gospel for All Contexts: Paul's Cross-Cultural Communication, by Chris Burnett

> **INSERT 12.1:** Birth of a Church: The Taliabo of Southeast Asia, by Stephen Lonetti
>
> **INSERT 12.2:** Evangelizing in the Shadow of the Vatican, by Massimo Mollica

CHAPTER 13: Sharing the Gospel with Jewish Friends, by Marty Wolf

> **INSERT 13.1:** The Importance of Israel and Jewish Evangelism, by David Zadok

Key Memory Verse

So faith comes from hearing, and hearing by the word of Christ.

—ROMANS 10:17

Additional Memory Verses

- Acts 17:30–31
- Romans 11:25–27
- 1 Corinthians 9:23
- 2 Corinthians 2:14–17
- 2 Timothy 4:5

Scriptures for Further Meditation

- Isaiah 52:13–53:12; Acts 14:8–20; 1 Corinthians 2:14; Hebrews 2:14–15

Summary of Textbook Content

Cultural engagement from the standpoint of the Great Commission requires a faithful presentation of God's Word. In particular, it is gospel proclamation and not cultural accommodation that the Lord uses to save the lost. Paul's interactions with both the Lycaonians and the Athenians display a proper and effective way to minister God's Word, and they establish a pattern for all missionaries to follow today. Whether one is witnessing to a Jewish unbeliever, a Roman Catholic, or a polytheist, it is the Word of God that must come to bear upon their unbiblical worldview.

Learning Objectives

- Understand cultural engagement from a biblical standpoint, and distinguish it from cultural accommodation.
- Recognize Paul's cultural engagement strategy with those in false religions who had not been reached.
- Understand the sufficiency of Scripture in gospel proclamation.
- Gain principles for effectively evangelizing people from different religious backgrounds (Roman Catholic, Jewish, tribal paganism).

> The straightforward words and concepts of the gospel, expressed in a linguistically understandable way with assertive force, are the Holy Spirit's weapons to disrupt all that is false in the belief system of the audience.
>
> **—Chris Burnett, "One Gospel for All Contexts: Paul's Cross-Cultural Communication"**

Recall and Reflect

1. Define biblical cultural engagement and biblical **cross-cultural communication**. [Burnett, "One Gospel for All Contexts"]

2. What are the three principles for biblical cross-cultural communication derived from Paul's letters? [Burnett, "One Gospel for All Contexts"]

3. What was it that prepared the Taliabo people to be receptive to the gospel? [Lonetti, "Birth of a Church"]

4. How did the missionaries display the love of Christ to the Taliabo people before they were able to communicate verbally to them? [Lonetti, "Birth of a Church"]

5. In what ways does the Vatican cast a long shadow over Italy? [Mollica, "Evangelizing in the Shadow of the Vatican"]

6. What is required for effective dialogue with a Roman Catholic adherent? [Mollica, "Evangelizing in the Shadow of the Vatican"]

7. What are some key messianic prophecies from the Old Testament to be aware of when evangelizing a Jewish person? [Wolf, "Sharing the Gospel with Jewish Friends"]

8. Why is it better to use "Messiah Jesus" instead of "Christ Jesus" when speaking with Jewish people? [Wolf, "Sharing the Gospel with Jewish Friends"]

9. What are the three recent "restorations" among the Jewish people that reflect God's preservation of them for their future, ultimate restoration? [Zadok, "The Importance of Israel and Jewish Evangelism"]

Analyze

1. In what ways might missionaries be tempted to read their local context into the text of Scripture? Why are cultural accommodation strategies of no benefit to the missionary?

> Truly, there is no greater privilege or joy than to share in gospel ministry and the advance of Christ's church.
>
> **—Stephen Lonetti, "Birth of a Church: The Taliabo of Southeast Asia"**

2. What faulty assumptions would motivate someone to refer to Jesus as the "Pig of God" in a Pacific Island context? What is the correct aim of faithful Bible translation that missionaries should strive for instead?

3. Because God's Word is central in the proclamation of the gospel, it is the missionary's greatest tool for reaching people. How is this assertion demonstrated from Scripture? How should the missionary's strategy be affected by this understanding?

4. Why do you think working through the Old Testament first before proclaiming Jesus Christ was an effective way of reaching many members of the Taliabo community?

5. How might a Roman Catholic misunderstand shared terminology such as "sin" and "repentance"?

6. What theological beliefs need to be removed from a Roman Catholic's thinking, and what theological beliefs need to be added? In other words, with what does a Roman Catholic need to be confronted, and with what does a Roman Catholic need to be presented?

7. Wolf explained that many Jews mistakenly believe that they are automatically Jewish from a religious standpoint simply because they were born into a Jewish family. How might understanding this misconception influence your evangelistic efforts toward Jewish people?

8. What are some historical reasons why Jewish evangelism has been neglected? What are some biblical reasons (include Scripture references) why it should not be neglected?

Implement

1. How might a missionary church leader help those like the Pacific Islanders understand Jesus as the Lamb of God?

2. Where would you take a Roman Catholic in Scripture if they said they were generally a good person?

3. How would you introduce and use Isaiah 53 in conversation with a Jewish unbeliever? Be specific. Where else might you take them in the Old Testament to further reinforce that Jesus is the Messiah?

4. If you were a missionary new to the field and were getting fresh exposure to cultural accommodation strategies, how would you "win back" a missionary or church leader who was promoting these strategies?

5. Lonetti's piece demonstrates that great patience is required for missionary work, and that it can take years of sharing the gospel before someone is converted to Christ. Is there anyone you have given up hoping would ever come to Christ? What can you do to cultivate a more persevering attitude of evangelism toward them?

Ask a Missionary

1. What strategies or methodologies have you seen on the field that are unbiblical and problematic for Christians? How have you seen unbiblical theological methodologies create confusion for Christians?

> Scripture alone convinced them of their sin and need for deliverance.
>
> **—Stephen Lonetti, "Birth of a Church: The Taliabo of Southeast Asia"**

2. What does biblical cultural engagement look like in your context, and how do you guard yourself against the temptation of altering Scripture to cater to the target culture?

3. In what ways have you had to engage in rooting out syncretism or exposing false beliefs and practices among professing believers in your context?

4. What language hurdles have you encountered when presenting theological terms or concepts in a foreign context? How have you been able to help your audiences have a clear and biblical understanding of these concepts?

5. What were some of the preliminary concepts and cultural connections you needed to understand and explain to ensure that your target audience could comprehend the gospel facts you were presenting? How long did that preliminary phase take, and what were some of the hurdles and pitfalls you encountered?

6. Before you were competent with the language and/or culture of the new mission field in which you were ministering, how were you able to reflect the love of Christ?

Study the Scriptures

1. Read Romans 11 in its entirety. What does Paul say concerning Israel's present spiritual condition as well as Israel's future spiritual condition?

2. Read Isaiah 52:13–53:12. Use a study Bible or commentary to learn the biblical interconnections and word pictures given there about the Servant of Yahweh. In what ways does this passage inform your understanding of Christ and increase your love for Him?

3. Summarize the messianic prophecies in the passages listed below. What additional prophecies do you think would be poignant in evangelizing a Jewish person? How might you introduce them in conversation with a Jewish friend? Use additional study resources to help.

A. _____   Isaiah 9:6
B. _____   Micah 5:2
C. _____   Isaiah 53:2
D. _____   Isaiah 53:4–9; Zechariah 12:10
E. _____   Isaiah 53:10
F. _____   Isaiah 53:11–12
G. _____
H. _____

4. How did Paul engage with the Lycaonians in Acts 14:8–20? How does this interaction inform biblical missions to pagan idolaters today?

5. How did Paul engage with the Athenians in Acts 17:16–34? How does this interaction inform biblical missions to the worldly wise today?

Missions Research

1. Research the Second Vatican Council and the impact **ecumenism** has had on the relationship between evangelicals and the Roman Catholic Church. What movements, events, organizations, or major documents have come about as a result? Describe them in chronological order. In what ways has this ecumenism shaped missionary work?

2. Compare and contrast the beliefs and practices that emanate from the worldviews of Southeast Asian animistic religions and African traditional religions. Populate the table below to compare their worldviews and practices. In the fourth column, state how the gospel directly confronts these systems.

Beliefs and Practices	Asian Animism	African Traditional Religions	Gospel Confrontation
Life after Death			
Guilt/Shame			
Prosperity/Health			
Deities			
Worship			
Sacrifices/Offerings			

> Jewish people are not unique in their need to be won to Christ, but they must be won uniquely. That requires knowing how they understand Judaism and how they view Christianity.
>
> **—Marty Wolf, "Sharing the Gospel with Jewish Friends"**

Application Projects

1. Choose a target people group whose language you can speak. Research a popular religion within that people group, identifying its major teachings about deity, man, sin, and the solution(s) to man's fallenness. Then design a gospel tract for adherents to that religion, a tract that you could print out from your home computer at low cost. Make it visually appealing, but focus on confronting the false worldview and faithfully, clearly presenting the gospel to your target audience with Scripture. Keep this tract for future use, improvement, or reuse, such as translating it or making it a template for other tracts.

2. Identify a religion that contains some overlap with Christianity, such as Roman Catholicism, Eastern Orthodoxy, Jehovah's Witnesses, Seventh Day Adventism, or Mormonism. In the space provided, compile a list of key biblical terms or concepts that are misunderstood in that religion. Identify and list which passages of Scripture you would use to clarify those terms and concepts. Then in a separate document create a lesson outline along with a handout for a Sunday school class or similar setting to explain how the target religion misunderstands the terms, the implications on its understanding of the gospel, and the correct biblical view. Cite your opponents accurately and fairly, and be winsome—they could be in your audience.

3. What could you teach to equip your congregation or small group for outreach to Catholics or Jewish people? In a separate document outline a four-week series on evangelism with texts, themes, recommended resources (that you have read), and discussion questions.

Living in Light of the Past

The History of Missions and Its Ongoing Legacy Today

Textbook Content

CHAPTER 14: Biblical Proclamation in Missions History: A Concise Reference Guide, by Chris Burnett

> **INSERT 14.1:** The Origins and Growth of the Church in India, by Sammy Williams

> **INSERT 14.2:** Recent Slavic Christian History, by Robert Provost

CHAPTER 15: Reformation Power: God's Word, a Light in Darkness, by Nathan Busenitz

> **INSERT 15.1:** William Carey and the Spark of Modern Missions, by Brad Klassen

> **INSERT 15.2:** Adoniram Judson: Reasons for a Lasting Impact on Myanmar Churches Today, by Silas Van Duh Hmung

Key Memory Verse

For God, who said, "Light shall shine out of darkness," is the One who has shone in our hearts to give the Light of the knowledge of the glory of God in the face of Christ.

—2 CORINTHIANS 4:6

Additional Memory Verses

- Psalm 119:105
- Psalm 119:130
- 2 Thessalonians 3:1
- Hebrews 4:12–13
- Hebrews 12:1–2

Scriptures for Further Meditation

- Psalm 78:5–8; Proverbs 6:23; Acts 6:7; 2 Timothy 2:2

Summary of Textbook Content

Modern missionaries can be encouraged by those who have gone before them. By also studying the historical developments in cultural engagement, missionaries and church leaders can be equipped to deal with problems today, such as in matters of missions strategy. Historically, the Reformation had a key role in bringing the church back to Scripture. The Reformers themselves, and many who followed their example of bold faith, had an undying commitment to the sufficiency and authority of the Bible. Missionaries today must share this same commitment to ensure success in the eyes of God.

Learning Objectives

- Trace the historical development of missions.
- Identify key missionary figures.
- Identify key doctrinal issues facing the task of missions.
- Understand the spectrum of cultural engagement in historical missions.
- Understand the centrality of the Word in forming and reforming the church.

> It was the ignorance of Scripture that made the Reformation necessary. It was the recovery of Scripture that made the Reformation possible. And it was the power of Scripture that gave the Reformation its enduring impact.
>
> **—Nathan Busenitz, "Reformation Power: God's Word, a Light in Darkness"**

Recall and Reflect

1. Which individuals practiced cultural accommodation in the third century, and how? [Burnett, "Biblical Proclamation in Missions History"]

2. Which third-century church father harnessed theology in line with **propositional assertion**? What was his "rule of faith"? [Burnett, "Biblical Proclamation in Missions History"]

3. What are four reasons to conclude a paradigm shift occurred in cross-cultural engagement during the Middle Ages? [Burnett, "Biblical Proclamation in Missions History"]

4. What hampered Clement of Alexandria in his communication of theology? [Burnett, "Biblical Proclamation of Missions History"]

5. How does Burnett describe the way in which Tertullian engaged in linguistic accommodation? [Burnett, "Biblical Proclamation in Missions History"]

6. In what ways did scholastic theology have a negative impact on the church in the High Middle Ages? [Burnett, "Biblical Proclamation in Missions History"]

7. Who were the first missionaries to India, and what did they do? [Williams, "The Origins and Growth of the Church in India"]

8. What caused the Protestant Reformation, according to Martin Luther? [Busenitz, "Reformation Power"]

9. What book by William Carey is considered the first theology of missions, known to be published in 1792? [Klassen, "William Carey and the Spark of Modern Missions"]

10. What three reasons does Silas Van Duh Hmung give for Judson leaving a lasting impact in Myanmar? [Hmung, "Adoniram Judson"]

Analyze

1. Regarding the spectrum of cross-cultural engagement, how would you explain the distinctions between Clement, Origen, and Felix on one side and Tertullian on the other?

2. How should the church respond within a culture that seeks to suppress the proclamation of God's Word?

3. Why was it important during the time of the Reformation for the people to have access to copies of Scripture?

> Judson's commitment to Scripture is also seen in his translation of the Bible into the Burmese language. He reasoned that winning people to Christ would require "distributing Bibles and tracts in every possible way, and in every language under heaven."
>
> **—Silas Van Duh Hmung, "Adoniram Judson: Reasons for a Lasting Impact on Myanmar Churches Today"**

4. How does using human reasoning as our ultimate authority oppose *sola Scriptura*? Be specific, using Scripture to support your answer.

5. How did William Carey's "convictions in the sovereignty of God and the obligation of His commission" allow him to persevere through "illness, loneliness, opposition, and the absence of conversions"?

6. What commitments compelled Adoniram Judson to translate the Bible into the language of the people?

7. Adoniram Judson was known for distinguishing between superficial interest in Christ and genuine salvation. Why is it important for the missionary to be cautious in affirming someone's salvation? Does this encourage or discourage people from genuinely following Christ? Explain your answer.

> If missionaries would see any genuine spiritual awakening among the unbelievers to whom they go, or any lasting revival in the weak or unhealthy churches to which they are called, it will not come through market-driven techniques or man-centered strategies. It will only come through the faithful preaching and teaching of the Scripture as the Spirit uses His Word to do a supernatural work in the hearts of people.
>
> **—Nathan Busenitz, "Reformation Power: God's Word, a Light in Darkness"**

Implement

1. When it comes to prioritizing the order of doctrine first and practice second, how do you intend to remain faithful?

2. What can you do to encourage spiritually immature or newly saved believers to have greater interaction directly with the Word of God?

3. Hmung highlights the rigorous preparation that Adoniram Judson went through before heading to the mission field, both academically and spiritually. In what ways do you personally need more preparation in order to have greater impact in ministry? What practical steps will you take to be more prepared in those areas?

4. Though William Carey trusted greatly in God's sovereignty and knew that the Word of God was the key to success, this did not diminish his commitment to personal diligence. Identify some areas in which you lack perseverance. What is the reason for this tendency (i.e., laziness, discouragement, distraction, etc.)? What do you need to do to maintain a more diligent attitude?

Ask a Missionary

1. In your context, how have you seen missions in the past continuing to bear fruit today?

2. What problems from missions in the past do you see recurring today?

3. How have you seen the providential hand of God overcome such problems in your context?

4. A continuous theme in the early church was an emphasis on the power of God's Word to transform lives. How have you seen that in your context?

5. What are some of the greatest discouragements you have faced on the mission field, and how did you overcome those discouragements?

6. Which missionary from church history has influenced you the most? Why?

Study the Scriptures

1. Study Acts 6:7; 12:24; 19:20. What do these passages describe as the source of the growth of the early church? Using a commentary or study Bible, list some synonymous expressions with Luke's use of the phrase "the word of the Lord" throughout Luke-Acts. What does this mean for the **global church** today?

2. Read Luke 24:13–49, with special attention to verses 27, 32, and 45. What does "He opened their minds to understand the Scriptures" mean? What are the theological implications of this?

3. Study 2 Corinthians 4:6. What is the "light" that "shall shine out of darkness"? What is the "Light of the knowledge of the glory of God"?

4. Study 2 Chronicles 35. What were the effects of Josiah's reformation? How did the Protestant Reformation parallel Josiah's reformation?

Missions Research

1. Research some of the influential missionaries in the history of your target nation or people group. Consider the following questions:
   a. Who were they, and where did they go?

   b. What activities did they do that can be identified as biblically faithful? Do you have concerns about any of their activities?

   c. What was the fruit of their work?

2. Pick one missions organization linked to one of the missionaries you researched. Using the diagram of the spectrum of cultural engagement (Fig. 6.1), plot the organization according to what most characterizes its mission and practice between the propositional or cultural accommodation models. On a separate sheet of paper, based on the data you gathered in the previous prompt, write out a few lines of rationale.

Figure 6.1

●– –●
propositional   **cultural**
(proclamation-oriented)   **accommodation**

3. Research the history of the Reformation or **Counter-Reformation** in either your country of origin or country of service. Then create a timeline presentation to trace this history backward from your family, a church, or a seminary of your choosing within that country to Europe at the time of the Reformation or Counter-Reformation in the sixteenth century. Plot significant dates with descriptions along the way. You might plot historical people, councils, confessions and creeds, institutions, monarchies, influential political events, translated works, denominations, or historic churches. Then answer the following questions in your presentation: In what ways does the Reformation's influence or lack thereof endure in your chosen country today? How has this strengthened or crippled the church and its mission there? What continuing reformation is needed in the church there today?

> Recognized today as the father of modern missions, he came on the scene in a period of evangelical lethargy. Paralyzed by hyper-Calvinism and apathy toward the lost, most English churches in the eighteenth century believed that if God wanted to save sinners, He would do so without their participation. Carey's life sparked a dramatic change.
>
> **—Brad Klassen, "William Carey and the Spark of Modern Missions"**

Application Projects

1. If you are a part of a missions organization, please answer these questions directly. If you are not yet engaged with a missions organization, research one you might partner with and answer these questions as if you were already a part of the organization:

   a. Who were the key founding members or institutions of your organization, what were their core theological convictions, and are they still upheld and applied on the field?

   b. What were their direct influences on your organization's ministry culture and philosophy?

   c. If you can identify where the theological and practical focus has changed, what do you perceive was the reason?

   d. If there is a need for corrective action to align your ministry with the biblically faithful pattern of ministry, what would be your objective process for addressing the areas of concern that you have identified? If there is no need for corrective action, what opportunities are there to strengthen the biblical pattern in your organization?

   e. How would you begin to inform or exhort the current leadership of your ministry in a manner that is productive and likely to create change toward the proclamation ministries evidenced by faithful missionaries throughout history?

2. Research the five *solas* of the Reformation. List them below, and write down key Scripture references for each. Write out specific ways that each *sola* ought to influence the practice of missions.

3. What challenges exist in your mission field (actual or potential) that are similar to the opposition the pre-Reformers and Reformers faced in their contexts? In the following table list your context's challenges, those of the pre-Reformers and Reformers, and the encouragement you draw from these comparisons. It may be helpful for drawing comparisons to identify categories of opposition (e.g., social, political) and specific pre-Reformers or Reformers individually (e.g., Jan Hus, William Tyndale).

Challenge	Your Context	Pre-Reformer/ Reformer Context	Encouragements
Social Opposition:			
Social Opposition:			
Political Opposition:			
Political Opposition:			
Other:			

Living in Light of the Future

Current Concerns in Missions and the Impact of Biblical Eschatology

Textbook Content

CHAPTER 16: The Consequences of a Compromised Commission: A Historical Analysis of Twentieth-Century Mission Theory, by Chris Burnett

CHAPTER 17: A Witness to the End: The Church's Mission in the Last Days, by John MacArthur

> **INSERT 17.1:** Endpoints Determine Midpoints, by Abner Chou

CHAPTER 18: Missions Today in Light of Christ's Imminent Return, by Chris Burnett

> **INSERT 18.1:** A New Creation Model for Today, by Michael Vlach

Key Memory Verse

Behold, I am coming quickly, and My reward is with Me, to render to every man according to his work.

—REVELATION 22:12

Additional Memory Verses

- 1 Thessalonians 5:4–6
- 1 Timothy 4:6
- 2 Timothy 3:12–14
- Titus 2:11–13
- Jude 24–25

Scriptures for Further Meditation

- 2 Corinthians 5:18–21; Philippians 3:20; Colossians 1:13–14; 2 Thessalonians 6:5–12; 2 Peter 3:13

Summary of Textbook Content

As the effectiveness of modern-day evangelical missions becomes increasingly diminished by ecumenical trends that cloud the mission of the church, believers must diligently cling to a biblical model of missions. A doctrinally precise understanding of the future is essential to be faithful to that cause. We must proclaim the gospel to the lost with a heightened sense of urgency since Scripture instructs us to anticipate the imminent return of Christ and His subsequent righteous judgment of all mankind. The times will go from bad to worse until that day arrives, so we must not be distracted by futile earthly causes that bear little spiritual fruit. A clear understanding of the future keeps us focused on what matters today: the faithful proclamation of Christ to those needing rescue from the wrath to come.

Learning Objectives

- Understand the risks and trends of compromise and confusion in missions.
- Recognize ecumenism, liberalism, and doctrinal drift in the church and in missions.
- Recognize the necessity for sound doctrine in missions practice of the future.
- Understand the role of biblical **eschatology** in fulfilling the church's mission.
- Analyze the impact of eschatological systems on missions strategies.

> The stakes underscore the urgency and eternal value of missions. God is establishing a kingdom for Himself out of every nation through the gospel of His Son. That kingdom, reflecting a multitude of cultures, languages, and ethnicities, will take part in glorifying the Son and the Father.
>
> **—Michael Vlach, "A New Creation Model for Today"**

Recall and Reflect

1. What have ecumenically oriented missiologists considered to be the primary goal of missions? [Burnett, "The Consequences of a Compromised Commission"]

2. What needs to be set aside in order to accomplish the goals of ecumenism, and how does this threaten the objectives of the Great Commission? [Burnett, "The Consequences of a Compromised Commission"]

3. What was the consequence of the failure to establish a doctrinal basis for partnership at the Edinburgh Conference of 1910? [Burnett, "The Consequences of a Compromised Commission"]

4. What position did the World Council of Churches take on missionary outreach? [Burnett, "The Consequences of a Compromised Commission"]

5. What Scripture shows that evangelism is not optional for the believer? [MacArthur, "A Witness to the End"]

6. What warning from Scripture about the direction of history in this age sharpens the necessity of the Great Commission? [Chou, "Endpoints Determine Midpoints"]

> The reality of Christ's imminent return and the coming of the end of the age ought to heighten our fortitude, increase our fervency, clarify our focus, and motivate our faithfulness. This kind of intensified approach to fulfilling the Great Commission becomes inevitable when our theology of missions is consistent with what Scripture reveals about the future.
>
> —John MacArthur, "A Witness to the End: The Church's Mission in the Last Days"

7. What is the motivation for boldness in proclaiming the gospel now? [Burnett, "Missions Today in Light of Christ's Imminent Return"]

8. What are the two broad, basic models of eschatology that have dominated since the second century AD? [Vlach, "A New Creation Model for Today"]

Analyze

1. Contrast mainline ecumenism and biblical unity. What is the difference, and why is this distinction important to understand for missions?

2. In Burnett's chapter "The Consequences of a Compromised Commission," he quotes John Stott's assertion regarding the Great Commission that "the actual commission itself must be understood to include social as well as evangelistic responsibility." What is your response to Stott's assertion?

3. How has the adoption of familiar evangelical vocabulary (e.g., *grace, peace, gospel, mission, justification, incarnation*) by heretical groups led to increased ecumenism?

4. How do Scripture's warnings that the world is getting worse, not better, compel missions rather than discourage them? How do they influence the missionary's goals and methods?

5. Why is it important for the missionary to understand that Christ is coming to bring universal, righteous judgment upon the earth?

6. How would you respond to a critique that dispensationalism means there should be no expectation of cultural transformation?

7. What are some ways in which false eschatological viewpoints tend to distract believers from what really matters?

8. What priorities would missionaries have if they sought to present the church as a spotless bride to Christ at His return?

Implement

1. How would you respond to someone who expresses that a diversity of views among elders in a local church regarding "secondary" doctrinal issues is ideal for biblical unity?

2. How does the thought of Christ's imminent return affect your life today? How would your life be different if you thought about this reality more frequently?

3. How might a clear understanding of the future help you to endure suffering in this present age, either now or on the mission field?

4. Consider some subtle ways you have seen unbiblical church growth methods creep into otherwise doctrinally sound churches. Why are these methods so tempting for missionaries? What biblical truths can you ground yourself in now to protect you from such temptation in the future?

5. Consider your long-term objectives. What current pursuits in your life are determined by those end goals? What pursuits are not but should be?

Ask a Missionary

1. How have you seen doctrinal compromise, if at all, in your context? How should Christians practically guard against deception, distortion, and compromise in the church?

2. How has sound doctrine worked to protect both your personal life and your public ministry?

3. What elements of **pragmatism** have you seen displayed in missions practice?

4. How do you maintain a sense of urgency in missionary work? What biblical realities push you to continually preach the gospel?

5. How have you seen a person's position on eschatology influence their view of missions? How has your eschatology informed your own practice of missions?

> Eschatology matters, because what a person believes about the end determines how they live today—what he invests in, strives toward, and focuses on. There should be no wonder, then, that a missionary's mindset, motives, and methods are directly or indirectly determined by his eschatology.
>
> **—Abner Chou, "Endpoints Determine Midpoints"**

6. What eschatological truths have helped those you've ministered to and in what ways?

Study the Scriptures

1. Study 2 Corinthians 5:11–6:10 using one or two commentaries of an **expositional** or applicational nature. What does it mean for Christians to be "ambassadors for Christ"? What is "the ministry of reconciliation"? What aspects of it compelled the apostles to endure such suffering as cataloged here?

2. Read 2 Peter 3 meditatively. List each time that an eschatological truth highlighted in this passage is intended to compel the believer's life today, and in what way.

3. Study the rapture of the church in 1 Thessalonians 4–5. How was Paul using this doctrine to encourage the Thessalonians? How does it serve as an encouragement to you today? What other passages highlight this same reality?

4. Read the letter of Jude. What does he mean by "contend earnestly for the faith" (v. 3)? What threat was there to the faith among the letter's recipients? What episodes or individuals from Scripture does Jude cite as being contiguous with this threat?

5. Read Isaiah 65–66 and Revelation 21. What truths contained in these chapters encourage you to persevere in your ministry efforts, and why?

Missions Research

1. Research the use of the terms ***missio Dei*** and *missional* in the missiology of three groups: Roman Catholic **inculturists**, ecumenical Protestants, and evangelicals. Begin by searching the conference papers, covenants, encyclicals, and journals cited in Burnett's chapters, "The Consequences of a Compromised Commission" and "Biblical Proclamation in Missions History." Then answer the following:

   a. How are the terms used by Catholics and ecumenists, and how do they compare or contrast to the uses of the terms by evangelicals?

   b. What strategies and practices do Catholics and ecumenists propose when using these terms, and how do they compare or contrast to the strategies and practices of evangelicals who use these terms?

2. Research the literature describing the "C1–C6 spectrum" of "**insider movements**," which reflects different kinds of Christ-centered communities in contexts of false religion, like Islam or Hinduism. Populate the levels of the spectrum in the following diagram, providing a brief description for each "C" level in the appropriate box. Then research a recognized insider movement in a context of your choosing and mark where it falls along the spectrum. In the space above the diagram, provide a rationale for your ranking by describing the activities of the movement that fit the given "C" level where you have placed it.

Figure 7.1

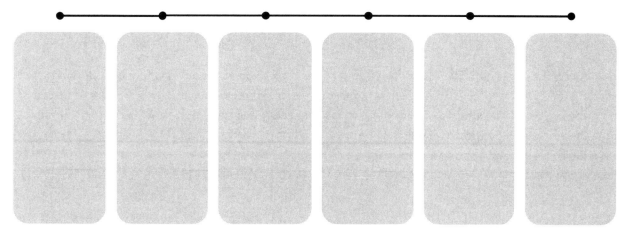

3. Explore the impact of the eschatological systems of futuristic premillennialism, amillennialism, and postmillennialism on missions activities. Find a missions agency subscribing to each of these systems. Start by reading agency statements of faith and the denominations of their sending and supporting churches. Then read up on the philosophy of ministry of each agency and the specific activities of their missionaries. Sketch a list of observations as to what differences in strategies and activities might result between the three systems.

4. Research the Edinburgh Conference of 1910. What were the objectives of the conference, and what were the outcomes? Why was this conference problematic for the practice of biblical missions and what problems have perpetuated until today?

Application Projects

1. In a separate document write out your own doctrinal statement on eschatology in a form you could hand to a potential supporting church or missions agency. Use a trusted systematic theology volume or two. Include in your statement at least three practical applications of your eschatological views on the cultural engagement activities you are currently doing or plan to do in the field. Describe these applications in detail.

2. How does your understanding of the kingdom of God affect your expectations for the following three points? After answering below, on a separate sheet of paper sketch an outline for a message that you could present to a Bible study or group of believers that addresses these points. Make sure to support your assertions with Scripture references.
a. Audience reception of the gospel message.

b. Social change (e.g., political, environmental, institutional policies).

c. Cultural development.

3. Suppose a national partner on the field has been taught that certain accommodation strategies, such as the rapid church-planting movement, are essential for ministry in the community. How would you lovingly push back on this assertion? Discuss with your ministry team (actual or potential) at least three questions to ask that relate to how the national partner defines the church and whether the accommodation strategies support the biblical Great Commission. Summarize your conclusions below. Then find a participant to role play how this conversation might go in person.

> Now is the right time to return to the basics of true kingdom work by following the footsteps of those missionary forebears who confronted false faith and presented the truth, preaching and teaching God's Word persuasively.
>
> —Chris Burnett, "The Consequences of a Compromised Commission: A Historical Analysis of Twentieth-Century Mission Theory"

Missionary Development Step 1
Identifying Missionaries for the Field

Textbook Content

CHAPTER 19: Igniting Passion for Missions in the Local Church, by Rodney Andersen

> **INSERT 19.1:** Priorities a Missions-Minded Pastor Needs to Have, by Paul Washer

CHAPTER 20: Mobilizing and Mentoring for Missions: Ten Key Considerations for Every Church, by Cecil Stalnaker

> **INSERT 20.1:** Psalm 67: Pray to Be a Blessing to the World, by Chris Burnett

Key Memory Verse

How then will they call on Him in whom they have not believed? How will they believe in Him whom they have not heard? And how will they hear without a preacher?

—ROMANS 10:14

Additional Memory Verses

- Psalm 67
- Isaiah 26:8
- John 4:35
- 2 Corinthians 5:14
- Revelation 5:9

Scriptures for Further Meditation

- John 4:23; 17:24; Acts 13:1–4; 1 Corinthians 11:1; Ephesians 1:4–6

Summary of Textbook Content

The missionary development process begins with igniting a passion for missions within the local church. This starts with the church's leadership. The elders must model through their lives a passion for Christ's glory in the world. This must be demonstrated through faithful preaching, consistent prayer, and strategic promotion of missionary endeavors. As a missions-minded culture begins to develop in the church, its leaders must also be diligent in the missionary selection and cultivation process, from examination and testing to mentoring and equipping. As the church maintains these pursuits, it will see the congregation as a whole cultivate an intercessory heart for the nations that aligns with God's redemptive purposes in the world.

Learning Objectives

- Explain why promoting missions and missionaries is vital to the congregation.
- Understand the priorities pastors need to have to be more missions-minded.
- Learn the necessity of adequately equipping missionaries before sending them to a foreign land.
- Learn how to identify, evaluate, and cultivate potential missionaries in the local church.
- Explain the need for learning cross-cultural skills.
- Recognize "mission drift" in the church and how to avoid it.
- Cultivate a heart of intercessory prayer for God's glory among the nations.
- Consider ways to cultivate a missions-minded culture across the entire church congregation.

> The local church carries the primary responsibility for mobilizing and mentoring missionaries to proclaim the gospel.
>
> **—Cecil Stalnaker, "Mobilizing and Mentoring for Missions: Ten Key Considerations for Every Church"**

Recall and Reflect

1. What relationship does prayer have with missions? [Andersen, "Igniting Passion for Missions in the Local Church"; Burnett, "Psalm 67"]

2. What specific steps can a local church take to promote missions? [Andersen, "Igniting Passion for Missions in the Local Church"]

3. When it comes to a church's support of missions what two things are inextricably linked? [Andersen, "Igniting Passion for Missions in the Local Church"]

4. Summarize the four P's that serve to ignite missions in the local church. [Andersen, "Igniting Passion for Missions in the Local Church"]

5. What are the consequences when the word "go" in Matthew 28:19 is underemphasized? What are the consequences when it is overemphasized? [Washer, "Priorities a Missions-Minded Pastor Needs to Have"]

6. What is the role of missions agencies in the support of missionaries? [Stalnaker, "Mobilizing and Mentoring for Missions"]

7. What is the role of the local church in the sending of missionaries? [Stalnaker, "Mobilizing and Mentoring for Missions"]

8. What should the local church consider when working with and choosing a missions agency? [Stalnaker, "Mobilizing and Mentoring for Missions"]

9. What should a missionary consider when choosing a country to serve in? [Stalnaker, "Mobilizing and Mentoring for Missions"]

10. How long did it take Paul before he began his missionary work? What example does this serve for missionaries today? [Stalnaker, "Mobilizing and Mentoring for Missions"]

Analyze

1. Why is it important for supporting churches to make regular visits to their missionaries?

2. Why should the church be the primary mobilizer for missions and not missions agencies?

3. What specific weaknesses in a missionary candidate would deem the candidate unfit for missionary work?

4. Why is it important that a missionary not be a new convert?

If leaders view missions support as just another side program of equal importance with the decorating committee, for example, the congregation's view of missions will be small as well.

—Rodney Andersen, "Igniting Passion for Missions in the Local Church"

5. Can you explain the relationship between desire and theological knowledge in missions? What problems arise when a candidate possesses desire but not theological training?

6. What are the potential consequences when a missionary team is not doctrinally united?

7. How do you think a small church can be faithful to the priorities of the Great Commission when it is still relatively young and lacking in resources, both financially and spiritually?

8. What are the internal and external elements of evaluating a missionary's call? What might be the consequences when each one is emphasized at the expense of the other?

9. What aspects of personal discipleship might be most effective for helping young people develop a biblical view of missions? State and explain at least three aspects.

Implement

1. What would you say to someone who asked you why the elders should be on the missions board at your local church?

2. What is your church doing currently to fulfill the priorities of the Great Commission? How could you personally contribute more to the fulfillment of these mandates?

3. Would you say that you maintain a heart for the nations that aligns with God's plan revealed in His Word? What can you do to further cultivate such a heart?

4. In what ways can you personally build relationships with existing missionaries on the field?

5. If you are considering going into missions, what should you begin doing today to start preparing spiritually, theologically, intellectually, materially, and culturally? Give a bullet-point answer to each of these aspects below.

Ask a Missionary

1. How were you discipled as a pre-missionary candidate?

> The Great Commission is urgent. The workers are few and the harvest is plentiful. But having more workers is not necessarily better, for a church's failure to carefully evaluate missionary candidates can cause significant damage to the cause of Christ. Testing and approval are critical because life and ministry become more complex and stressful in cross-cultural contexts.
>
> **—Cecil Stalnaker, "Mobilizing and Mentoring for Missions: Ten Key Considerations for Every Church"**

2. Did you go to seminary or Bible school before going to the mission field? Where did you go, and how did that institution prepare you for missions? If you did not go, how did you prepare theologically before leaving?

3. What would you say to the pre-missionary candidate who desires to go into missions but does not yet have biblical and theological training?

4. What shortcuts have you observed missionaries making, and how have those shortcuts negatively affected their gospel ministry?

5. What do you see being done well in missions today? What do you see being done poorly?

6. What impact does your Christian character have on your credibility on the mission field?

7. How is church reproduction envisioned and pursued at the church where you are currently serving?

Study the Scriptures

1. What does it mean to worship "in spirit and truth" (John 4:23)? To inform your answer, use a concordance or Bible search engine to survey John's uses of these terms (*pneuma* and *alētheia*, respectively) throughout his New Testament writings. How is it that the Father is "seeking" worshipers?

2. Do some journaling on Psalm 67. What observations can you make regarding the psalmist's prayer? What are his motivations and desires? Memorize the psalm, and pray its themes each day for two weeks. Then journal again describing what impact the psalm has had on you, along with any potential answers to prayer you have seen.

3. What patterns for missions training can be drawn out of 1 Timothy 3:10 and 5:22 and their contexts? When and how might a "testing" period be incorporated into the missionary appointment and sending process?

4. Reread Acts 13:1–4. What were the four activities being done by the church leaders, Paul, and Barnabas before the latter were "sent away" in missions (vv. 2–3)? Which activities did they do in response to the Holy Spirit's calling? Are you doing likewise in your own preparation for missions, whether you are the one sending or the one being sent?

Missions Research

1. Research the prayer theology and practices in the lives of three missionaries. Choose from William Carey, Hudson Taylor, Adoniram Judson, Amy Carmichael, Jim and Elisabeth Elliot, Anthony Norris Groves, George Müller, Samuel Zwemer, or others who have surfaced in the textbook. In the space provided, identify a few commonalities in their convictions about and practices of prayer. Then also state any unique findings about their attitudes toward prayer.

2. What are the best resources for facilitating informed prayer for **unreached people groups** and restricted access countries, whether in print or online? In a separate document create a list of effective tools for praying intelligently and accurately for missions that you could access during your own prayer times or share with others. In your compilation, be sure to consider the research methods, theology, and missions philosophy promoted by the toolmakers.

> The result of planting and pastoring a local church is that some who are trained by the missionary will become the pastors and others will go out to plant new churches. They will evangelize, disciple, and raise up elders elsewhere among their people and beyond. This is the cycle of biblical missions—the outworking of the Great Commission.
>
> **—Paul Washer, "Priorities a Missions-Minded Pastor Needs to Have"**

Application Projects

1. How can you emphasize global missions in your local church beyond an annual missions month or Sunday? On a separate sheet of paper, draft a proposal to address or engage missions in the following outlets of regular church life:

a. Sunday services

b. Sunday classes

c. Midweek fellowship groups (home Bible studies, small groups)

d. Children's and youth ministries (Sundays, midweek, vacation Bible school, camps, and retreats)

e. Communication platforms (bulletins, emails, social apps)

f. Prayer meetings and events

2. Plan a hypothetical missions conference, one like the annual conferences many churches host. Include in your plan such things as a conference site, date(s) on your church's calendar, schedule, theme, keynote speakers and texts, seminar topics and speakers (chosen from the missionaries sent or supported by your church), Q&A participants and topics, book promotions, giving emphasis, and so on. Put your plan together in a master document or spreadsheet organized and presentable enough to be shared with a leader.

3. Make a list of ministry and personal needs of missionaries, as found in their newsletters or as reported by supporting churches. Write down each missionary's name, the country or region where they are serving, the category of need (emotional, material, physical health, personal, family, team, institutional, etc.), and, using Scripture, record how you plan to pray for or practically meet the needs.

Missionary's Name and Location	Category of Need	How to Pray	How to Practically Meet Their Need

4. Complete the missionary candidate questionnaire, titled "First Step Information". This real questionnaire, created by one local church's missions leadership team, is a sample list of interview questions you can expect a church to ask you if you apply for missionary support. Complete the form as if you were in the candidating process.

FIRST STEP INFORMATION

Your name (and immediate family members and their relationship to you):

Our church's missions leadership team would like to learn some things about you. Please complete the questions below and return to our teammate who oversees missionary care and development. Your answers do not have to be detailed—just the basic data. Once the form is completed, we can set up a time and date to talk further. One of our teammates will go over the questions with you.

─────────────── **Questions** ───────────────

1. In what year and what city were you born? (If your citizenship is in another country other than your place of birth, please indicate.) Where do you consider home?

2. Provide your mailing address, phone numbers, and email address.

3. Tell a little about your family situation (if married, names of spouse and children, children's ages, years married, and any other thing you think might be important in relation to your family).

4. What are you currently doing (e.g., school or work—you and your spouse)?

5. What prior schooling have you had? Have you graduated from a Bible college or seminary? If so, which school and when did you graduate? (If you are currently a student, state your year and when you plan to graduate.)

6. How did you become a follower of Jesus Christ (you and your spouse—just looking for a paragraph or two from each of you at this stage)?

7. What church do you currently attend, if not ours? For how many years have you attended this church? Are you a member? If applicable, do you attend a Sunday morning fellowship group or class? Please provide the name of the church, its address, and pastor's name.

8. Is the church that you attend and its leadership aware of your interest in missions? What is the leader's name who is aware of your interest?

9. In what type of ministries are you currently involved inside and/or outside of the local church?

10. What is your current involvement with unbelievers?

11. Briefly describe your gifting, talents, or strengths that will enhance your ministry.

12. As far as you know, are there any circumstances that might keep you from serving the Lord in ministry (health, family, large consumer debt, large college loans, etc.)?

Questions 13–20 are only for those *not* returning to their country of citizenship (i.e., missionaries).

13. At this time, how strong is the conviction you (and your spouse) have to ministry overseas? If you were to rate it on a scale of 1 to 10 (10 being the strongest), how would you rate your conviction? Your spouse's conviction? Why?

14. How long have you each been interested in missions?

15. When it comes to serving the Lord overseas, is there a particular location in the world and type of ministry you'd like to be involved in? Why? Does anybody on the field of your interest know about this?

16. What length of service are you interested in?

17. What do you look forward to in ministering overseas and cross-culturally? What are you anxious or fearful about?

18. Do you have an idea when you would like to arrive on the mission field? State the approximate month and year.

19. Describe your thoughts and feelings about raising your own prayer and financial support.

20. If you are from a church other than ours, please provide information about this church (city, state, country, church name, denomination, etc.). Do you believe they will be your sending church?

_____ **Questions 21–27 are for those returning to their** _____
country of citizenship (i.e., national partners).

21. If you are desiring to return to your country of citizenship, explain why you believe that it would be beneficial to come under the authority and accountability of our missions leadership team and elders rather than returning without this relationship.

22. Were you sent here from a church in your country of citizenship? If so, please provide information about this church (city, state, country, church name, denomination, etc.). Are they supporting your studies? Do they want you to return to that church upon the completion of your studies?

23. Is your primary desire to be involved in translation work, church planting, pastoral training, or other type of ministry? Please explain.

24. Describe your thoughts and feelings on raising prayer and financial support.

25. How long would you estimate that it would take for a church plant in your country to become self-sustaining?

26. What do you look forward to in ministering in your country of citizenship? What are you anxious or fearful about?

27. Do you have an idea when you would like to return to your country? State the approximate month and year.

Missionary Development Step 2

Preparing Missionaries for the Field

Textbook Content

CHAPTER 21: Courage to Carry Out the Great Commission: Missionary Calling, Competence, and Character, by E. D. Burns

> **INSERT 21.1:** Living on the Brink of Eternity: The Life of David Brainerd, by Brad Klassen
>
> **INSERT 21.2:** Where Are You on the Spectrum of "Suffering for Jesus"? Brief Examples from the Field, by Kevin Edwards
>
> **INSERT 21.3:** The Accumulation of Small Sufferings, by Brooks Buser
>
> **INSERT 21.4:** Missions Includes Missionaries with Disabling Conditions, by Dave Deuel

CHAPTER 22: The Elder-Qualified Missionary: Preparing Missionaries to Plant Churches and Train Others on the Field, by Tom Pennington

CHAPTER 23: Nonoptional Pre-field Training: Biblical Doctrine, by Chris Burnett

Key Memory Verse

Be diligent to present yourself approved to God as a workman who does not need to be ashamed, accurately handling the word of truth.

—2 TIMOTHY 2:15

Additional Memory Verses

- Luke 9:23–26
- 2 Corinthians 12:9–10
- 1 Timothy 3:1–7
- 2 Timothy 2:24–26
- Titus 1:5–9

Scriptures for Further Meditation

- Acts 20:27–28; 1 Timothy 3:10; 2 Timothy 2:1–6; 3:12; 4:7; 1 Peter 4:10

Summary of Textbook Content

Missionaries face a vast array of potential hardships on the mission field, such as false teaching, relational challenges, persecution, financial difficulty, and sickness, just to name a few. Because of the immensity of the task before them, missionaries must be carefully vetted and thoroughly equipped by their sending church before they ever reach the mission field. This preparation must include doctrinal clarity, personal character, and practical skills. Missionaries must be thoroughly grounded in an unshakable reliance on the sufficiency of Scripture, for God's Word is the only clear guide for all the hurdles that lie ahead. Ultimately, the responsibility to prepare the missionary lies squarely with the local church. To neglect this responsibility is to set the missionary up for failure and to poorly steward the Great Commission mandate.

Learning Objectives

- Understand the New Testament pattern of raising up faithful elders in the local church.
- Obtain a practical process for training elders.
- Grasp the contribution of each major doctrine of systematic theology to missions.
- Grasp the centrality of the local church in preparing missionaries.
- Understand the reality of persecution and hardship while persevering to boldly preach the gospel.
- Appreciate models of missionary sacrifice throughout church history.

> Despite their zeal to obey the Lord's command in the Great Commission, churches must never compromise on the qualification and preparation of the ones they send to fulfill it.
>
> —Tom Pennington, "The Elder-Qualified Missionary: Preparing Missionaries to Plant Churches and Train Others on the Field"

Recall and Reflect

1. What are the eight roles that the apostle Paul charges Timothy to have? [Burns, "Courage to Carry Out the Great Commission: Missionary Calling, Competence, and Character"]

2. What are four character qualities of the slave of Christ required for a missionary? [Burns, "Courage to Carry Out the Great Commission: Missionary Calling, Competence, and Character"]

3. What label did J. C. Ryle give to the distaste for doctrine among the missionaries of his day—and why did he call it that? [Burns, "Courage to Carry Out the Great Commission: Missionary Calling, Competence, and Character"]

4. Explain the difference between teaching and correcting. [Burns, "Courage to Carry Out the Great Commission: Missionary Calling, Competence, and Character"]

5. What are the three biblical truths Deuel highlights that prove that believers with disabilities can and should pursue missions in whatever way they are able? [Deuel, "Missions Includes Missionaries with Disabling Conditions"]

6. What is the biblical argument for the role of pastor/elder being restricted to qualified men? [Pennington, "The Elder-Qualified Missionary"]

7. What four areas should elders desiring to raise up future elders focus on? [Pennington, "The Elder-Qualified Missionary"]

8. Why does Burnett argue that biblical doctrine is nonoptional pre-field training? [Burnett, "Nonoptional Pre-field Training"]

> Missions work involves two things that last forever—the Word of God and human souls.
>
> —E. D. Burns, "Courage to Carry Out the Great Commission: Missionary Calling, Competence, and Character"

9. What are the eleven categories of systematic theology? Name and briefly explain each. [Burnett, "Nonoptional Pre-field Training"]

Analyze

1. What does it mean for missionaries to have "doctrinal courage"? Why is it important for missionaries to possess this trait?

2. Why is handling adversity one of the greatest factors in determining whether someone is fit to serve on the mission field?

3. Why is the accumulation of smaller forms of suffering often harder to endure than major sacrifices? How does this affect your view of missionary work?

4. What are some unique opportunities and advantages that people with disabilities have in doing missions work?

5. What is the role that a seminary has in equipping elders in contrast to the local church?

6. How might a missionary's view of the gifts of the Holy Spirit affect their approach in missions?

7. How do the biblical doctrines of anthropology and **hamartiology** affect how the missionary engages the culture?

8. How does **soteriology** shape a missionary's gospel proclamation?

9. Why is it both unbiblical and unproductive to consider sinners "pre-Christians"?

10. The following table is intended to represent how a missionary's core commitments to service are informed by biblical doctrine (**orthodoxy**) and lead to sound missions practices (**orthopraxy**). The first column lists the commitments and the second column represents the doctrinal categories most closely associated with them. Reference the chapter "Nonoptional Pre-field Training: Biblical Doctrine" to complete the table:

Missionary Commitment	Category of Theology	Key Scripture Reference(s)	Missionary Practices
Literal, grammatical, historical interpretation	Bibliology		
Expository preaching and teaching	Bibliology; soteriology; ecclesiology		
Modeling holiness and making disciples	Soteriology; anthropology; ecclesiology		
Training and establishing elders	Ecclesiology		

a. In the third column, provide key Scripture references from the associated doctrine(s) that undergird the commitment in the first column. Where more than one doctrinal category is associated, provide at least one reference for each.

b. In the fourth column, indicate specific missionary methods or ministries that directly result from the theological commitments in the first column.

Implement

1. Elders/Pastors: Evaluate the current missionaries your church supports. Do they meet the biblical qualifications to be on the field? If not, what growth needs to occur in them? How do you plan on assisting them in that goal?

2. Elders/Pastors: What training program do you have in place for elder candidates? If you do not have one, what steps should you take to put a program in place?

3. How would you begin the process of confronting a missionary on the field who exhibits disqualifying behavior or doctrine?

4. If someone were to ask you how women can qualify to be on the mission field even though women cannot be elders, how would you respond?

5. How would you encourage believers with disabilities to serve the Lord in the local church? If you have a disability, in what service can you take along others who do too?

6. How would you respond to someone who argues that training in biblical doctrine is not essential for the missionary?

7. How are you responding to the cost of discipleship today as presented by Jesus in Luke 9:23–27, 57–62?

8. List the various sufferings that David Brainerd endured during his missionary career. How did he respond to those difficulties? How can you prepare yourself now for sacrifices in the future?

Ask a Missionary

1. How do the people in your target culture understand genuine kindness?

2. What role does patience play in your missionary efforts? How has patience benefited you on the mission field?

3. Are there any biographies that have uniquely inspired you as a missionary?

> Sacrifice comes in many forms. It is usually not at the end of a weapon, but rather in the simple things where a follower of the King lays down his life in ways that are never printed in a support letter.
>
> **—Brooks Buser, "The Accumulation of Small Sufferings"**

4. What aspects of missionary work have been the hardest for you to endure? Which ones have been the most challenging for your spouse or children? How have you and your family overcome those difficulties?

5. How have you experienced suffering or persecution on the field? Have the people you have seen come to faith experienced persecution or suffering? What effect has this had on their discipleship?

6. What mistakes have you seen on the field that, in your opinion, were the result of insufficient pre-field missionary training? What aspects of training would you consider essential for future missionary partners (yours or another's) to have?

7. Why is it important for missionaries to be familiar with each category of systematic theology? What examples come to mind?

Study the Scriptures

1. Read the story of Paul's shipwreck in Acts 27–28. Make a list of all the adverse circumstances that Paul encountered. Based on these chapters, what should you expect as a gospel ambassador on the mission field? How do you think you would respond if all of this happened to you today?

2. Read and consider each passage under the heading of **bibliology** or a category of systematic theology of your choosing as laid out in Burnett's biblical doctrine chapter. Summarize the implications these passages have on missions.

3. Using the notes of a good study Bible, examine Deuteronomy 6:4; Isaiah 48:11–16; Matthew 28:19; John 1:1; Acts 5:3–4. What do these passages tell us about the nature of God? How can these truths shape our missiology?

4. Read Hebrews 6:10; Luke 18:28–30; Revelation 22:12. How do these passages encourage you to persevere in hardship?

5. Do a study in Scripture on the impact of serving in ministry while being biblically disqualified. Consider biblical characters and groups, such as Nadab and Abihu, Hophni and Phinehas, the prophet Hananiah, Judas, or former ministry partners of Paul like Hymenaeus, Alexander, and Philetus.

Missions Research

1. Look up the ten countries where Christians are most persecuted and list them below. What are common characteristics of the persecution in these areas? Pick one or two of these countries and conduct further study to see the state of the church there. Then make a separate list of ways to pray for the local churches there personally and with your prayer partners.

2. Study the life of a historic missionary such as John G. Paton, David Brainerd, Amy Carmichael, Gladys Aylward, or Adoniram Judson, whose ministries were marked by suffering. Write an essay that answers the following questions:

a. How were the biblical qualifications for spiritual leadership (1 Tim 3:1–7; Titus 1:6–9) evidenced in his or her life and ministry? How might those qualifications have enabled perseverance in ministry while suffering?

b. What did he or she say about suffering and persecution, either as biblical instruction or as statements about personal experiences? What Scriptures did they draw from?

c. Cite specific situations in the missionary's life in which he or she demonstrated faithfulness to these principles in times of suffering and persecution.

3. Compare the doctrinal statements of three **parachurch** ministries that conduct ministry in your mission field (actual or potential). Then on a separate sheet of paper do the following:

a. Draw up a table and collocate their theological expressions by major doctrinal category, including "prolegomena."

b. Identify differences between the doctrinal statements, such as comprehensiveness, ambiguity, reliance on historic creeds or confessions, conflicting positions between them, and so on.

c. Identify differences between the ministry priorities and activities of each organization as reported in their own words (website, print literature, missionary newsletters).

Application Projects

1. Team conflicts are among the primary reasons for teammates leaving the field. List the biblical texts about unity and harmony that you are committed to employing and maintaining on the mission field with team members. If you are on a team (in ministry or in training) or in a class, make this a group activity with discussion.

2. The mission field magnifies a person's personal struggles and temptations, often in a context where there is less help available and little opportunity to receive the comfort and rest needed for dealing with personal problems.

a. Create a personal evaluation of how you handle adversity generally.

Answer the following questions:

• What specific hardships do you have the most difficulty handling (e.g., sickness, physical pain, rejection, criticism, inconvenience, discomfort, stress, financial hardship, temptation)?

• How do you normally respond when you face those scenarios?

- What is the perspective of those who are closest to you (e.g., spouse, children, close family members, and friends) about how you handle difficulty? Ask them to be honest and thorough and summarize their responses. Do not attempt to defend yourself in response.

b. Based on this evaluation, on a separate sheet of paper create a targeted plan for growing in those areas.

Include specific answers to the following questions:

- What sinful attitudes and patterns do you need to put off (Col 3:9), put away (Eph 4:31), or lay aside (Rom 13:12; Eph 4:22, 25; Col 3:8; Heb 12:1; James 1:21; 1 Pet 2:1)? What do you need to put on (Eph 4:24)?

- Share your plan with those who are close to you, perhaps those who already provided you a personal evaluation. Ask for their feedback on how you can improve it. Ask them to pray for you and hold you accountable. Record their feedback below.

3. Missionaries, like all believers, can be accused of not practicing what they preach. To avoid the common accusation of hypocrisy, how can missionaries intentionally live the same gospel principles they preach in the context of their family, team, and leadership relationships? Fill out the following chart to link specific attributes/perfections of God in Scripture to the gospel message a missionary must proclaim on the basis of these truths. In the last column, be specific about how a missionary should aim to live out each aspect of godly character in his or her most important relationships.

Missionary Development Step 3

Sending Missionaries to the Field

Textbook Content

CHAPTER 24: Church Elders and Missions: Evaluating and Planning a Missions Program in the Local Church, by Tom Pennington

CHAPTER 25: Don't Hand Them Off: The Ongoing Role of the Home Church in the Life of a Missionary, by Rodney Andersen

    INSERT 25.1: Supporting Your Church's Missionaries, by Tom Pennington

CHAPTER 26: Gospel-Centered Prayer: Paul's Priorities in Colossians 4:2–6, by Mark Tatlock

CHAPTER 27: Seven Ways to Pray for Missionaries, by John Glass

CHAPTER 28: Shrewdly Investing in the Great Commission: The Parable in Luke 16:1–13, by Eric Weathers

    INSERT 28.1: The Place of Paul's Letters in His Missions Efforts, by Dave Deuel

    INSERT 28.2: Best Practices for Effective Support-Raising Letters, by Santiago Armel

Key Memory Verse

I thank my God in all my remembrance of you, always offering prayer with joy in my every prayer for you all, because of your fellowship in the gospel from the first day until now.

—PHILIPPIANS 1:3–5

Additional Memory Verses

- Romans 15:30–32
- 2 Corinthians 9:7–9
- Philippians 4:19
- Colossians 4:2–6
- 1 Thessalonians 5:25

Scriptures for Further Meditation

- 2 Corinthians 8:7–9, 22–24; 1 Thessalonians 5:17; James 5:16; 1 Peter 5:1–4

Summary of Textbook Content

Local churches have a critical role in the missionary endeavor. The elders of the local church must exercise diligent oversight over its missions efforts and have an ongoing shepherding and counseling role for those who are sent out to the field. Church members can also wisely steward their financial resources to supply necessary funding for ongoing missions efforts. Ultimately, any success on the mission field is the outcome of diligent gospel-centered prayer. Missionaries must learn how to communicate effectively with both their sending churches and their supporters, understanding the essential role they play.

Learning Objectives

- Identify the local church elders' role in providing oversight of their church's missions program.
- Consider ways that a church can provide ongoing care for both the missionary and his family.
- Understand the nature of financial and other types of support.
- Understand how to effectively fundraise and communicate with supporters.
- Understand how to pray effectively for missionaries.
- Consider key factors when assessing compatibility with a missions agency.
- Recognize the necessity of depending on God in prayer to accomplish the work of missions.
- Identify ways to use finances for the advancement of the gospel.

> Christ's followers must prayerfully decide how they can best honor Him with their money from an eternal perspective. There is perhaps no better way to do this than by investing in the advancement of expositional preaching in both local and global contexts, so that individual congregations are equipped by their pastors to do the work of the ministry for generations.
>
> —Eric Weathers, "Shrewdly Investing in the Great Commission: The Parable in Luke 16:1–13"

Recall and Reflect

1. What are the three criteria for developing an effective missions grid that church leaders can use when evaluating missionaries to support? [Pennington, "Church Elders and Missions"]

2. What are six unique ways that elders and pastors can support their church's missionaries? [Pennington, "Supporting Your Church's Missionaries"]

3. What function does a missions leadership team perform, and why is it important? [Pennington, "Church Elders and Missions"; Pennington, "Supporting Your Church's Missionaries"]

4. What must a church not abdicate when utilizing parachurch ministries like missions sending agencies? [Andersen, "Don't Hand Them Off"]

5. What are several purposes of Paul's letters to the churches? What does his letter writing indicate about Scripture's ability to be effectively communicated outside of the pulpit? [Deuel, "The Place of Paul's Letters in His Missions Efforts"]

6. What is the missionary's primary support need? [Armel, "Best Practices for Effective Support-Raising Letters"]

7. What is the important point that Jesus teaches his followers in Luke 16? How does this apply to believers? [Weathers, "Shrewdly Investing in the Great Commission"]

8. What were Paul's two requests in Ephesians 6:19? What does this tell us about the duty of the local church? [Glass, "Seven Ways to Pray for Missionaries"]

9. Summarize the seven aspects of Paul's prayers noted in Glass's chapter. [Glass, "Seven Ways to Pray for Missionaries"]

Analyze

1. Why is it important for a church to have criteria for supporting missionaries and ministries? What kind of criteria should be used?

2. Why is it vital that missionary qualifications for church planting or pastoral training roles be the same as elder qualifications? What are the implications or consequences if they are not?

3. Why is prayer so indispensable to the fulfillment of the Great Commission?

4. How might a missionary communicate to his supporters in a way that points them to God and His glory rather than to himself?

5. What is the relationship between the messenger of God and the message from God? What are the implications of this concept in preaching today?

6. What factors should be considered when determining to work with a missions agency, and why?

7. How are "watchfulness" and "thanksgiving" related to each other in the context of prayer?

Implement

1. What aspects of ministry might you be neglecting in prayer? For whom or what do you need to pray more consistently, and how?

2. How do Paul's prayers from various New Testament passages influence you to pray for your brothers and sisters in Christ? How about those on the mission field? Be specific.

> Knowing that many people pray for their missionaries daily, it is reasonable to perceive that gospel opportunities are the direct result of an army of saints praying for open doors of ministry.
>
> **—John Glass, "Seven Ways to Pray for Missionaries"**

3. How does it encourage you to know that even Paul requested prayer that he would be courageous enough to open his mouth to speak the gospel with boldness? What does this communicate about your own dependency on prayer for gospel ministry?

4. Every believer in the local church needs to "hold the rope" in support of missionaries that have been sent out by the church. How can you personally help to "hold the rope" for a supported missionary in your church?

5. How might you steward your wealth toward the Great Commission? How would go about deciding where to allocate your wealth?

6. If you run a business or manage a company, how might you promote a focus on the Great Commission in your workplace?

7. With Paul's letters as an example, how might you utilize letter writing as a way to edify believers and advance the gospel?

Ask a Missionary

1. What are some of the most helpful ways that supporting churches have encouraged your ministry?

2. What methods did you use to raise support? Which ones were the most helpful in your view? About how long did it take you to be adequately funded for departing to the field?

3. What advice would you give to new missionaries for utilizing their gifts and time most effectively on the field to glorify God?

4. What is your strategy for communicating with supporters? How do you keep them engaged with your ministry and encourage their ongoing prayer support?

5. Do you work with a missions agency? If so, what support does the agency offer in addition to your sending church? Have you had any difficulty working with missions agencies in the past?

6. What are some ways you have seen God answer prayer on the mission field?

7. What are the areas in which you or your family need prayer the most?

Study the Scriptures

1. Read the book of Philippians as you would a letter. How does Paul reflect on the Philippians' support of him? What exhortations and teachings struck you as relating to the church and missions?

2. Study Acts 6:1–7, in particular the priorities that the apostles highlighted in verse 4. Why is prayer highlighted alongside service of the Word as the most indispensable priorities for church leadership? Do you think prayer receives as much emphasis as the service of the Word in your church's missions today? Why or why not?

> Missionaries may have thousands of dollars in monthly resources, but if
> churches are not praying for them, they really have no support.
>
> **—Santiago Armel, "Best Practices for Effective Support-Raising Letters"**

3. Study Nehemiah 2:4–8; Isaiah 41:10; Philippians 4:11–13; and 1 Timothy 5:18, as collated in Armel's insert, "Best Practices for Effective Support-Raising Letters." What do these passages have in common? How do they assist the missionary in the formation of a budget?

4. In Colossians 4:5–6, Paul says that wisdom is necessary to have a good testimony before unbelievers and grace is necessary to know how to respond to them. One might assume the opposite, that grace is needed for a good testimony and wisdom is needed to know how to respond. Why do you think Paul phrased this passage the way he did?

5. Study the context of the following passages: Acts 14:27; 1 Corinthians 16:9; 2 Corinthians 2:12; and Colossians 4:3. What does Paul mean by "a door," and how did this drive his actions/decisions in each context? What do these passages reveal about how Paul viewed and engaged in ministry?

6. Read Proverbs 11:14; 15:22; 24:6; and Luke 14:28–32. What do these texts say about the importance of human planning and having an abundance of counselors? How does this apply to preparing for the mission field?

Missions Research

1. Research the history of the concept of "faith missions" and the principles behind this approach. Start with the life and writings of Anthony Norris Groves (1795–1853), and describe his influence as the "Father of Faith Missions." Define his approach to missions and two or three ways in which it is prevalent still today.

2. Trace the shift in the authority of the local church over missionary service by researching the history of "missions/missionary societies." Look for the role local churches played in the formation of those societies, particularly as written about in missiology journals between 1985 and 1995. Summarize your findings in chronological order below.

3. Many local church leaders today do not consider themselves missions experts or authorities. Investigate the policies of three major missions agencies, and state how they express the role and authority of the local church in the life of the missionaries they support.

4. Research Christian benefactors known for giving away the majority of their resources for global missions. Identify two of them and list key principles that drove them to extreme giving to advance the Great Commission.

Application Projects

1. Read the full doctrinal statement of your local church or, if applicable, your sending church. Then research various sending agencies to evaluate which agency is most aligned with your church's convictions. Create a presentation identifying potential sending agencies that your church would be able to partner with, which you could offer to present to an elder at your church and solicit feedback.

2. Come up with a creative strategy to utilize your finances to advance the gospel, following these steps:
   a. Consider whom you could reach out to in order to begin this process. List the name of the missions pastor, elder, or missions leadership team member in your church whom you could ask about specific needs or outlets of which they may be aware. Summarize their advice.

b. Investigate some potential giving opportunities by gathering information from Christian publishers, Bible translators, missions agencies, and other parachurch organizations that prioritize proclamation ministries. List your favorite options and why.

c. Investigate a few like-minded **indigenous** leaders who regularly train men for pastoral ministry, whom you might meet at conferences, seminars, or church events, or whom you might seek out by contacting them directly. Ask about specific needs they may have, offering to pray for them but being careful not to commit financial giving yet. Summarize your findings.

d. In a separate document or spreadsheet, draft a budget (as a family, if applicable) for giving to the advance of the gospel, and meet again with your missions leader for input on communicating it appropriately to the recipients. Then be faithful and prayerful (as a family) in meeting your budget and sending the funds.

3. One local church has designed the "missions support grid" in Figure 10.1 for determining how to steward their financial resources effectively for their missionaries. It is presented as a template for discussion and potential use with local church missions leadership teams. Discuss the following questions with a partner or group, and summarize your conclusions:

a. What categories of the grid are new for your church?

b. Which of the components would your team consider adopting?

c. What percentages would you adjust differently for the various categories?

d. In what specific ways does this grid prompt you to pray differently for your local church, your missions leadership team, and your missionaries?

Figure 10.1

Sample Missions Support Grid

		Ministry Focus						
		Least Reached, Church Planting, or Leadership Development			Missionary Support, Discipleship, or Church Support Activity			
		Missionary	Ministry Focus	Annual Support	Missionary	Ministry Focus	Annual Support	
Relationship to Church	Homegrown and Home Church	Missionary A	Church Planting	-	Missionary H	Missionary Pilot	-	
		Missionary B	Leadership Development	-	Missionary I	Missionary Teacher	-	
	Home Church	Missionary C	Leadership Development	-	Missionary J	Prison Ministry	-	
		Missionary D	Leadership Development	-				
	Related Home Church	Missionary E	Church Planting	-	Missionary K	Bible Translation Support	-	
	Unrelated Home Church	Missionary F	Church Planting	-				
		Missionary G	Leadership Development	-				

	Grid Level	Beginning Support Level	Support Level Cap	Grid Level	Beginning Support Level	Support Level Cap
Grid Guidelines	1	-	-	5	-	-
	2	-	-	6	-	-
	3	-	-	7	-	-
	4	-	-	8	-	-

Populate the annual support, beginning support level, and support level cap in the supporting church's national currency.

4. Draft a thank-you letter to donors (actual or hypothetical) who have helped support your ministry financially. Then ask your local church's missions leadership team if you can help write ten thank-you letters to donors on behalf of the church's missions program, its **short-term ministry** teams, or its supported missionaries. Handwritten letters are preferred, if possible.

5. For this assignment, consider that you have been delegated by your local church's missions leadership team to visit one of the missionaries on the field whom your church supports. Use the following sample policy, and design your trip with the help of one of your church's missions leadership team members. Outline your trip details in a separate document.

A Policy for Missionary Leadership Visits

Please read the following policies and complete the questions at the bottom.

Purpose:

To intentionally provide encouragement, support, and accountability to our missionaries through regular leadership visits.

Our intent is to regularly visit each missionary who does not live locally.

1. These visits should allow the leadership to see the missionary engaged in his regular ministry and also to participate with the family in their regular, day-to-day life.
2. Visits should be made by a non-family elder, missions leadership team member, or other designated member.
3. Visits should not typically include any short-term missions team or ministry focus, since that would change the dynamic of the visit (it may be possible, however, for leadership to stay a few days after a short-term trip to have this time with the missionary).
4. Visits should be followed up by a report to the missions leadership team.

Frequency:

1. Missionaries for whom we are their sending church: once every three years
2. Missionaries for whom we are not their sending church: once every five years

Participants:

The leader to make these visits will be prioritized as follows:

1. The elder who works most closely with that missionary and their care team
2. Another elder on the missions leadership team
3. Another elder not on the missions leadership team
4. A non-elder missions leadership team member

5. Another member as designated by the missions leadership team

Finances:

From our short-term trip budget will be designated a set maximum financial amount of _____ (in our currency) for an international trip and of _____ (in our currency) for a domestic trip, to cover the following expenses:

1. The travel expenses, including meals, of the elder, missions leadership team member or other designated member
2. The travel expenses, including meals, of a spouse, provided the visit is to a missionary couple or single woman serving on the field (allowing a second elder's travel expenses and meals to be covered at the discretion of the missions leadership team if a spouse is unable to participate)
3. Any meals provided for the missionary family
4. A small gift for the missionary family (e.g., a family activity, something for their home)

Unique circumstances requiring a larger budget (such as more expensive flights, inability to stay with the missionary, etc.) must be approved by the missions leadership team. Please submit the following information to your elder or missions leadership team member:

- The name of the missionary you plan to visit
- Your relationship to the missionary, including how long you have known him or her
- What you hope to accomplish and how you plan to do it
- An explanation of any spiritual gifts that the elders recognize you as having that will contribute to the goal of the visit
- A description of any ways your visit might create a burden on the missionary and what you believe you can do to turn a burden into a blessing

LESSON 11

Caring for Missionaries on the Field
Meeting Needs

Textbook Content

CHAPTER 29: It's More Than Money: How to Support Missionaries on the Field, by Rodney Andersen

> **INSERT 29.1:** Creating a Missionary Care Team in the Supporting Church, by Tom Pennington
>
> **INSERT 29.3:** What Local Church Missions Leadership Needs, by Rodney Andersen

CHAPTER 30: Holding the Rope: 3 John for Missions Donors, by Eric Weathers

Key Memory Verse

You will do well to send them on their way in a manner worthy of God. For they went out for the sake of the Name, receiving nothing from the Gentiles. Therefore we ought to support such men, so that we may be fellow workers with the truth.

—3 JOHN 6–8

Additional Memory Verses

- Proverbs 17:17
- Galatians 6:2
- Ephesians 6:18–20
- Philippians 2:3–4
- 2 Thessalonians 3:1–2

Scriptures for Further Meditation

- 1 Corinthians 12:26–27; 16:15–18; 2 Corinthians 9:10–15; Titus 3:13–14

Summary of Textbook Content

A missionary's supporters are true partners in ministry. The Great Commission mandate would not be possible without them. There are a wide variety of ways to support missionaries that extend far beyond financial assistance. Members of a sending church can form teams aimed at caring for the missionary's practical, emotional, and spiritual needs. This can take the form of ongoing communication, personal visits, prayer, and the meeting of various physical needs. Personal relationships should be pursued so that such needs can be both understood and cared for.

Learning Objectives

- Understand the biblical precedent of churches caring for missionaries beyond financial support.
- Identify practical ways that churches can care for missionaries.
- Gain a method for organizing missionary care teams with defined responsibilities.
- Distinguish responsibilities between sending churches, supporting churches, and missions agencies.
- Assess missions agencies according to biblical fidelity and compatibility.

> The work of missions is not accomplished by the missionary alone, but in partnership with supporting churches.
>
> **—Rodney Andersen, "It's More Than Money: How to Support Missionaries on the Field"**

Recall and Reflect

1. How can the sending church and the missions agency clarify their respective roles so the missionary doesn't receive conflicting counsel? [Andersen, "It's More Than Money"]

2. While missions agencies do not have the primary role in sending missionaries, how might they provide key guidance to the missionary? [Andersen, "It's More Than Money"]

3. What is a missionary care team? [Pennington, "Creating a Missionary Care Team in the Supporting Church"]

4. What are the four essential components a church's missions leader should have? [Andersen, "What Local Church Missions Leadership Needs"]

5. If missionaries who are geographically separated from their sending church still need pastoral care, whose responsibility is it to provide such care, and why is it necessary? [Andersen, "What Local Church Missions Leadership Needs"; Andersen, "It's More Than Money"]

6. Who ought to be "fellow workers with the truth" according to Weathers? How do they perform this function? [Weathers, "Holding the Rope"]

7. In the book of 3 John, what are the three reasons why Christians should support missionaries? [Weathers, "Holding the Rope"]

Analyze

1. How might a missionary's relationship with his supporters be impacted if he views them as "fellow workers with the truth" (3 John 8)? How might that influence his communication with, attitude toward, and thoughts of them?

2. How should a missionary pray for his supporters?

3. Describe the ways in which Gaius supported the Great Commission as presented in 3 John.

4. How do individuals like Diotrephes serve as a threat to Great Commission efforts? How might believers vigilantly guard themselves and the local church against people such as Diotrephes?

5. Why is it important for a local church's missions pastor to visit the church's missionaries in their countries of service?

6. Why do missionaries need ongoing spiritual care, and what are some specific examples? Why are the elders of their sending church best suited to provide such care?

7. Why is it insufficient to provide spiritual care for a missionary and not his wife? What unique encouragement needs do missionary wives face on the mission field?

Implement

1. Does your church have missionary care teams assigned to the missionaries it supports? Summarize what they do to care for the missionaries, or else how your church cares for missionaries instead. How might you join them?

2. In what ways does your church help support missionaries who are on furlough? What are some spiritual needs your church can help meet? What about physical needs?

3. What are some ways your church supports its missionaries' family members living near the church, such as aging parents or children at university? Can this be improved?

4. How might your church best encourage its women on the mission field?

5. What does it look like to send missionaries "in a manner worthy of God" (3 John 6)? What are some ways you can better achieve that standard?

6. How can you personally guard against a Diotrephes-like attitude in your own heart? How can you protect the church from such an attitude?

> Leading the church in missions requires a passion for the work of Christ around the world. A lack of excitement about the work of missions will quickly become evident to others. Leaders without zeal will, by example, quench the congregation's enthusiasm about the global advance of the church.
>
> **—Rodney Andersen, "What Local Church Missions Leadership Needs"**

Ask a Missionary

1. How have the elders from your sending church been able to shepherd you from afar?

2. How has your sending church communicated with you on the field? What ideas would you recommend to churches who need advice on regular communication with their missionaries?

3. What advice would you give to church members on how to be better supporters for missionaries?

4. What areas of care do you feel are most likely to be neglected by sending/supporting churches?

5. Tell us how you feel about furloughs. Are they helpful or stressful for you? Why? If married, how do your spouse and children (if any) feel about furloughs?

6. Explain the role distinctions between missions agencies you work with and your sending church. Have you experienced any tension between them? How have you navigated that?

Study the Scriptures

1. Read Galatians 6:2. What does it mean to "bear one another's burdens, and so fulfill the law of Christ"?

2. Do a biographical study of Epaphroditus in Philippians 2:25–30 and 4:18. What is it about him that was such an encouragement to the apostle Paul? Describe the relationship between Paul, Epaphroditus, and the Philippian church outlined in this letter.

3. Based on the text of 3 John, create a brief biographical sketch comparing and contrasting Gaius and Diotrephes. What role do these two individuals play in the overall message of the book? What are the implications for missions today?

4. Research passages in which Paul requests prayer for his missionary endeavors, such as Ephesians 6:19–20; Philippians 1:19–20; Colossians 4:3–4; 2 Thessalonians 3:1–2; and others. What burdens seem to frequently preoccupy the apostle? How do these passages inform you about how to be praying for missionaries you support?

5. Consider the following table from 3 John compiled by Eric Weathers. Fill in the Scripture references using only your Bible, corresponding to the descriptions provided. Would you add to these? Be careful to draw from the specific language of the verse, using caution not to insert opinions or ideas that do not pertain to the passage.

Donors Holding the Rope for Missionaries	Passage
Christians must pray like the apostle John for the Lord to prosper donors who labor in support of missions.	3 John 1–4
Believers, like Gaius, must sustain the work of the Great Commission.	
A portion of the believer's hard-earned resources should be stewarded toward the Great Commission.	
It is okay for others to testify of a donor's love for missions and missionaries.	
Christians must support missionaries in a way that is worthy of God Himself.	
Marketplace Christians are morally obligated to help fund the Great Commission.	
Marketplace income producers who donate toward the Great Commission are known as, "fellow workers with the truth."	
All Christians must heed warnings about missions.	
Believers must not imitate men like Diotrephes who refused to support missionaries.	
Demetrius is a reminder to manifest the truth with a reputation for doing good.	

Missions Research

1. Research how missionaries were supported during the modern era of missions, particularly from the mid-eighteenth to nineteenth centuries. On a separate sheet of paper, create a list of ways that home churches and historic Protestant missionary societies contributed to the funding and care of field workers. Describe what you learn about the relationship of support and accountability between missionary societies, home churches, and missionaries.

2. Find some additional resources such as websites, articles, and print books that recommend best practices for communication between supporters and missionaries. What strategies and technologies do they present as most effective, and how do these compare with those suggested in the *Biblical Missions* textbook? Do any seem unbefitting? If so, how, and how can this be avoided?

3. To understand some of the emotional and spiritual challenges missionaries face, read resources in print or online that are related to the topics of cross-cultural adaptation, culture shock, missionary kid life, loneliness, grief, and ministry fatigue, among other topics. Then do the following tasks:
   a. Recount five real stories presented in those resources of challenges posed to missionaries.

   b. Write out the best way to overcome these challenges biblically, either suggested by the resources you read or gleaned from your own study.

> God does not call or equip every Christian with the needed skills for preaching His Word, for planting churches, or for training indigenous leaders on the mission field. But He does equip every Christian for ministry. In particular He equips some to "hold the rope." He gifts them with marketplace abilities to generate income—income that can be used for international missions.
>
> **—Eric Weathers, "Holding the Rope: 3 John for Missions Donors"**

Application Projects

1. In a separate document draft a statement that could be used by your local church or ministry partners that explains the primary role the sending church has in the missionary's shepherding, doctrinal accountability, and evaluation of ministry qualification. Ask your local church's missions leadership team or an elder to read it and give you feedback.

2. In a separate document, prepare a message that you might present to a local church ministry (e.g., adult Bible study, youth group, fellowship group, children's class) to motivate believers to pray for and support missions. Outline two versions of the same message, one of them being ten minutes long, geared either toward younger audiences or a devotional setting at church events, and the other being thirty minutes long with more detail, geared toward older audiences or more teaching-focused settings. The message can be topical or passage-based, but be sure that in both versions it exposits Scripture accurately, enlists supporting passages, and illustrates appropriately for its audience.

3. Find and read newsletters from ten current missionaries serving in different parts of the world. Then prepare a survey report that addresses the following questions without naming the missionaries or identifying your answers with any particular field:

a. What common prayer requests, burdens, and needs do missionaries tend to share no matter their context?

b. Which of the missionaries' concerns on the field might suggest the need for more effective pre-field preparation by the local church leadership? Explain what additional training might help future missionaries better deal with concerns on the field.

c. If you could "read between the lines," what kinds of struggles do you perceive the missionaries might have that they would not likely share with a wide audience? Offer suggestions on who might engage them with personal communication and how that might be done.

d. Let this survey inform your own prayers and preparation for or participation in missions. Then offer to share it with the missions leadership team at your church.

Shepherding Missionaries on the Field

Supporting Families

Textbook Content

CHAPTER 31: Shepherding the Family on the Mission Field, by Mark Borisuk

> **INSERT 31.1 SOCIOCULTURAL CHALLENGES TO THE MISSIONARY FAMILY IN COLUMBIA, BY SANTIAGO ARMEL**
>
> **INSERT 31.2:** Survey of Top On-Field Family Shepherding Issues, by Chris Burnett
>
> **INSERT 31.3:** Prayer and Care for Missionary Families, by Lauren Brown

CHAPTER 32: A Deadly Enemy of Faithful Missionaries: Love of Material Comfort, by Luis Contreras

> **INSERT 32.1:** Living in the Joy of Missions: An Antidote to Burnout, by Rick Kress
>
> **INSERT 32.2:** Ministering the Word in a Time of Crisis: A Pastor's Report from Ukraine, by Oleg Kalyn

Key Memory Verse

For the love of money is a root of all sorts of evils, and some by aspiring to it have wandered away from the faith and pierced themselves with many griefs. But you, O man of God, flee from these things, and pursue righteousness, godliness, faith, love, perseverance, gentleness.

—1 TIMOTHY 6:10–11

Additional Memory Verses

- Ephesians 5:22–6:4
- Philippians 4:12–13
- Hebrews 13:5–6
- 1 Peter 1:1–9
- 1 Peter 3:1–12

Scriptures for Further Meditation

- Proverbs 3:13–15; 15:16; John 10:11–13; Colossians 3:18–21; 1 Timothy 6:17–19

Summary of Textbook Content

A family living according to God's design is a life-giving aroma that may draw people to Christ. However, missionary families face acute challenges requiring abundant grace and support. A wide range of spiritual, emotional, and relational dangers threaten to undermine their effectiveness. Missionaries must be prepared to battle the temptations they will face, including materialistic longings, ministry burnout, and external crises. Senders must understand the challenges missionaries and their families encounter, and they should know how to shepherd them through them while practically caring for their ongoing needs.

Learning Objectives

- Understand the role of God's biblical design for the family in promoting the gospel.
- Identify and seek to address common challenges faced by missionary families.
- Learn practices for effectively supporting and caring for missionaries.
- Recognize the dangers of materialism and the biblical means to avoid it.
- Grasp the sources of joy necessary for enduring hardship.
- Realize that faithfulness intensifies through crisis rather than weakening.

> Going to the mission field or accepting the title of missionary does not spiritually transform a family into one that is ready to face the challenges of missionary life. On the contrary, perhaps nothing so quickly reveals the continued need for sanctification than being placed in a foreign culture.
>
> **—Mark Borisuk, "Shepherding the Family on the Mission Field"**

Recall and Reflect

1. Why must the missionary never neglect to shepherd his own family if he hopes to be successful on the mission field? [Borisuk, "Shepherding the Family on the Mission Field"]

2. What are four pieces of critical instruction that Proverbs gives for wise parents? [Borisuk, "Shepherding the Family on the Mission Field"]

3. Why is it crucial for a new missionary family to be spending as much time as possible with the nationals rather than the international community when arriving on the mission field? [Borisuk, "Shepherding the Family on the Mission Field"]

4. What are the four categories of top on-field shepherding issues that missionaries most frequently deal with? [Burnett, "Survey of Top On-Field Family Shepherding Issues"]

5. What is the greatest challenge a church faces in caring for its missionaries? [Brown, "Prayer and Care for Missionary Families"]

6. What attitudes lead to distrust in God's provision? [Contreras, "A Deadly Enemy of Faithful Missionaries"]

7. What are the three vital encouragements for living in supernatural joy that Peter gives believers in 1 Peter 1:1–9? [Kress, "Living in the Joy of Missions"]

8. How can the missionary grow in joy for the Lord on the field? [Kress, "Living in the Joy of Missions"]

Analyze

1. What are the roles of husband and wife in a biblical marriage?

2. What are the unique challenges that missionary kids face on the mission field?

3. Why is it important for God's people to be involved in fellowship? Why is this so important on the mission field?

4. What are some practical steps a missionary can take to unify his family before they head to the mission field?

5. Why does Scripture oppose the love of money, and why does it encourage believers to examine their hearts as it relates to money?

6. In what ways might missionaries be uniquely tempted by the lure of comfort?

7. How should a missionary determine an appropriate standard of living on the field?

8. Why must a church not deviate from **expository preaching** even during a crisis?

9. In what ways do you think suffering enhances a pastor's preaching ministry?

Implement

1. Has your ministry involvement threatened the quality of your relationships at home? How have you disciplined yourself not to neglect shepherding your own family even during busy seasons of ministry?

2. Describe what your own discipleship looks like. Who are your mentors? How often do you seek them out, and for what reasons? If you are married, what about your spouse? Is there anything you should do to more proactively pursue discipleship?

> Precise preaching and personal application in conjunction with a holy testimony in the missionary family are two catalysts for a nation's transformation.
>
> —Santiago Armel, "Sociocultural Challenges to the Missionary Family in Colombia"

3. Parents, how do you decide whether to send your kids to either public school or private school? Describe the factors that influence your decision. Would this change on the mission field?

4. How are you presently protecting yourself from ministry burnout, and in what ways can you further guard against it? Be specific.

5. Think about one individual (missionary, pastor, etc.) who is at risk of ministry burnout. What is one practical way you can encourage that individual?

6. What disciplines can you implement in your personal life to cultivate contentment rather than looking to possessions for satisfaction?

Ask a Missionary

1. If you have had children on the mission field, how did you go about spiritually discipling them in a new cultural context? What advice do you have for families embarking overseas?

2. How did your children adjust to life on the mission field? What helped and what hindered their transition?

3. Have you needed to care for aging parents while serving overseas? If so, how did you manage that responsibility?

4. What kinds of crises or hardships has your church faced over the years? How have you attempted to shepherd people faithfully through them?

5. What advice would you give to a prospective missionary regarding the lure of material comfort that can compete with ministry?

6. Have you established any financial accountability measures to safeguard your ministry? If so, what have those entailed?

Study the Scriptures

1. Study 1 Timothy 3:4–5 and explain how this passage could qualify or disqualify a man from greater ministry positions within the church. Then list at least three fathers from Israelite history who were in some kind of spiritual leadership but failed to lead their households well. How does Scripture comment about or characterize their poor example in this regard?

2. Reread 1 Timothy 6:6–11 and 17–19. What does it say about the proper place of money in contrast to the love of money? Scour the Bible for other wisdom on the subject, consulting a topical Bible or concordance. Make a list for personal use of the pertinent passages from Contreras's chapter "A Deadly Enemy of Faithful Missionaries" and the other passages you find.

3. Compare the truths contained in the following passages: Proverbs 3:13–15; 8:10–11; 15:16; 16:16. How do these verses help a missionary—who is dependent on others for income—maintain the right perspective on the mission field?

4. Carefully read Deuteronomy 4:9; 6:4–9; and 11:18–21. How does this instruction for Israel apply to the Christian family today as seen in New Testament passages like Ephesians 6:4? How might this kind of home also bear fruit for the ministry in a field that is hostile to public evangelism?

5. Study John 10:11–13, as mentioned in Kalyn's insert "Ministering the Word in a Time of Crisis." How would this passage be uniquely applicable when ministering to a church in crisis—to the church and to the missionary family? What types of sacrifice does it demand in your life today?

Missions Research

1. Research the concept of "third-culture kids" in both missiological and social studies. Then complete the following prompts:
   a. Specify the most common spiritual, emotional, and material needs that they face.

   b. Choose one mission field and identify the top sociocultural challenges it presents to the spiritual growth of children.

   c. List practical ways parents, local churches, and supporting churches can meet these common and context-specific needs.

> Whatever one may face—whatever failure, whatever sin, whatever victory, whatever success, whatever disappointment—the Christian's ultimate confidence is the saving mercy of God in Christ—nothing more and nothing less. Praise God for the basis of the sinner's salvation—sovereign, saving mercy through the person and work of Jesus Christ!
>
> **—Rick Kress, "Living in the Joy of Missions: An Antidote to Burnout"**

2. Find out what schooling options exist for missionary children in a country of your choosing. Note that you will have to survey the country as a whole, likely more than just one target people group. Survey the internet profiles of the schools and/or news articles featuring their methods within the country. Use a translator on your internet browser if you have to. List the pros and cons for each option available, considering differences in children's ages, personalities, learning disabilities, special needs, and so on.

a. Boarding school.

b. Homeschool.

c. Public school.

d. Private/international school.

3. Research burnout as a cause for missionary attrition cited within evangelical journals, agency reports, or missions society databases. Does the literature rightly identify the problem? How about the solution? What factors may be contributing to this more recent topic of discussion?

Application Projects

1. Choose a country, preferably a country you are interested in serving or currently serve, and consider what particular sins dominate its culture. Then create a counseling strategy by answering the following tasks in the space provided:

a. List the culturally prominent sins you observe.

b. List the Scripture passages you would need to confront each of those sins when evangelizing and discipling in that cultural setting.

c. Pick at least two of those sins and list specific ways that believers in that cultural context can fight temptation practically.

d. Write out prayer prompts to help you pray for believers in that cultural context as they fight temptation.

2. Personal struggles affect a minister's ability to serve in purity and complete devotion and are usually exacerbated in a new or foreign context. Fill in the table, which captures the following information:
   a. Some temptations you struggle against in your current context.
   b. Ways those temptations might worsen if you were to relocate to a new context.
   c. What "means of grace" you expect to help combat, abate, and eradicate any impurities that result when you fall to temptation. Some means of grace include Scripture reading, Bible and theological study, expository preaching, prayer, worship, spiritual fellowship and accountability, and the serving of others in ministry.
   d. Initial ideas about how to employ these means of grace practically.

Temptation	Ways it could worsen	Means of grace to address it	Action steps with this means of grace

3. Consider these difficult situations that can occur in the mission field: a church split, denominational infighting, personal accusations, and calamitous circumstances. How should a missionary husband shepherd his wife in the midst of attacks that come against him, her, or their family? How should a missionary wife comfort and protect her husband or their family? Write a letter to your spouse (actual or potential) with a detailed response to these questions that reflects your commitment to serve your family in the face of one or more of these situations. If married, share the letter and keep it in a special place where both of you can find it in the days ahead.

Starting Right

Biblical Parameters for Church Planting

Textbook Content

CHAPTER 33: Church Planting by the Book, by Stephen Lonetti

> **INSERT 33.1:** Partnering in Church Planting: The Benefits of a Shared Ministry, by Eduardo Izquierdo and David Perez

CHAPTER 34: Essential Principles for Church Planting, by Carl A. Hargrove

> **INSERT 34.1:** Doing the Work of an Evangelist, by John MacArthur

CHAPTER 35: The Joys of Planting a Church, by Conrad Mbewe

> **INSERT 35.1:** Church Planting in Post-Calvin Geneva: A Personal History, by John Glass

Key Memory Verse

And in this way I make it my ambition to proclaim the gospel, not where Christ was already named, so that I would not build on another man's foundation; but as it is written, "They who had no declaration of Him shall see, and they who have not heard shall understand."

—ROMANS 15:20–21

Additional Memory Verses

- Acts 2:41–47
- 1 Corinthians 3:6–7
- Ephesians 3:20–21
- Ephesians 4:11–13
- Colossians 1:28–29

Scriptures for Further Meditation

- Acts 14:21–23; Philippians 1:3–5

Summary of Textbook Content

The planting of new churches has a critical role in fulfilling the Great Commission. However, contemporary models of church planting deprioritize the preaching and teaching of Scripture. The faithful proclamation of the truth, cultivation of new disciples, and development of qualified leaders can be tiresome and time-consuming. Paul's personal example, as well as that of many modern-day church planters, demonstrates the great costs involved in planting a church. Yet the joys of partnership in ministry, advancement of the gospel, and growth of new believers are well worth the price.

Learning Objectives

- Grasp the definition and objectives of a church, including maturity and reproducing.
- Understand biblical church planting and distinguish it from unbiblical models.
- Comprehend the essential, biblical qualifications of a church planter.
- Anticipate the inevitable hardships and conflicts in the church-planting task.
- Formulate an initial philosophy of ministry toward church planting.
- Discern when and how to commission, send, and support church planters.

> A spiritually healthy church grows from spiritually healthy Christians.
>
> **—Stephen Lonetti, "Church Planting by the Book"**

Recall and Reflect

1. How is *church* biblically defined? [Lonetti, "Church Planting by the Book"]

2. What are Lonetti's four hallmarks of a mature church? [Lonetti, "Church Planting by the Book"]

3. What are the five steps of the birth and development of a church plant? [Lonetti, "Church Planting by the Book"]

4. What is the main cause of communication gaps in a gospel presentation? [Lonetti, "Church Planting by the Book"]

5. What are Hargrove's nine essential principles required for biblical church planting? [Hargrove, "Essential Principles for Church Planting"]

6. Name one significant error in recent church planting. [Hargrove, "Essential Principles for Church Planting"]

7. What are the eight steps in the church planting pattern of Paul at Ephesus? [Hargrove, "Essential Principles for Church Planting"]

8. According to MacArthur, what is the hard part of ministry, and why? [MacArthur, "Doing the Work of an Evangelist"]

9. What three obstacles does Mbewe identify that prevent churches from planting other churches? [Mbewe, "The Joys of Planting a Church"]

10. What type of perspective is required to be a church involved in planting other churches? [Glass, "Church Planting in Post-Calvin Geneva"]

Analyze

1. Why is it important for the Christian to communicate biblical concepts and definitions clearly to unbelievers?

> A ministry that honors the Master is marked by fidelity to Him, His Word, and the ministry objectives laid out in Scripture.
>
> —John MacArthur, "Doing the Work of an Evangelist"

2. Why is it important for a church plant to begin with a high view of God? In what ways will this attitude strengthen the church?

3. What are the risks involved if a church planter is not commissioned by a local church?

4. What challenges do church planters face when dealing with a postmodern relativist worldview?

5. Why might a pastor neglect doing the work of an evangelist, and what are the consequences of this neglect?

6. Why is being a biblically qualified elder the first requirement for a prospective church planter?

7. What is the biblical case for churches to prioritize planting other churches?

8. Lonetti states that teaching redemptive narratives is an effective way to lay a foundation for the gospel. Why are redemptive narratives particularly helpful for understanding the gospel?

9. What is the relationship between the edification of believers toward spiritual maturity and the extension of the gospel to the lost?

Implement

1. Lonetti rightly states that apathy, distraction, and theological weakness have a devastating effect on the church and that weak churches send weak missionaries who plant weak churches. How might you as a pastor, missionary, or church member assist in reversing these weaknesses? How do you ensure this does not occur in your own church?

> A church must never commission a man who needs to be convinced that he is the right person to meet some need. A man may need encouragement for the task ahead, as it may seem overwhelming to him, but a burden for the people must reside deeply within him.
>
> **—Carl Hargrove, "Essential Principles for Church Planting"**

2. If churches should only commission qualified individuals to plant new churches, what steps can you take today to become the type of person your church could legitimately send for a church-planting mission?

3. Pastors, what first step can you take to better incorporate an evangelistic mindset into your weekly work and church life?

4. How can you help your local church to grow beyond focusing on temporal needs in prayer meetings to prioritizing God's kingdom through missions?

5. In what ways do you need to cultivate prayer in your current ministry efforts? What should you be praying for more often?

6. Which people in your life today do you currently have a burden to reach with the gospel?

7. How might you go about constructing a team for a church plant?

Ask a Missionary

1. Describe how your local church helped prepare you for the mission field. What were the benefits of that preparation?

2. What biblical and unbiblical church growth movements have you seen on the mission field?

3. What steps did you take or are you taking to equip the indigenous members of your church to take over the ministry after you? What challenges have you faced in that process? What lessons have you learned?

4. Did you plant a new church or join an existing church? If you planted a new church, what were the biggest challenges you faced during the initial years? What encouraged you to persevere?

Study the Scriptures

1. What unique instruction does each of the following verses offer concerning preaching and teaching?
   » Matthew 28:20
   » Mark 16:15
   » Acts 5:42
   » Acts 10:42
   » Acts 15:35
   » Acts 28:31
   » Romans 15:20
   » 1 Corinthians 1:17
   » Ephesians 3:8
   » 1 Timothy 5:17
   » 1 Timothy 6:2
   » 2 Timothy 4:2

2. Read Acts 5:29–32; Galatians 1:10; and 1 Thessalonians 2:4. What do each of these passages present respectively as their bases for pleasing God rather than men in ministry?

3. Evaluate the following passages: Matthew 18:15–20; Acts 2:41–42; Colossians 4:12; 1 Timothy 5:9; Hebrews 10:24–25; 13:17. How might these passages be used to support the idea of church membership? Are there any other places you would go to in Scripture to defend the practice of church membership?

4. Study the four imperatives Paul gives to Timothy in 2 Timothy 4:5. In light of the context, why would Timothy need to be exhorted specifically in these four areas? Before you answer, read two or three commentaries on this and the surrounding verses to remind you of the situation and flow of the letter.

Missions Research

1. Research the contemporary "house church" movement that is popular in many countries and contexts. Then complete the following tasks:

   a. Present two contemporary house church models and summarize their characteristics, including the doctrinal statement and distinctives, leadership structure, meeting objectives, and activities.

   b. Present and summarize two traditional local churches that also seek to follow the biblical model from the same respective regions as the house church models listed in task a.

   c. Compare and contrast these findings on a separate sheet of paper. Create a three-column table that represents the contemporary house church's "pros," "cons," and any areas of concern (spiritual or practical).

> Most churches see themselves as the end of the chain, rather than as runners in the middle of a relay—runners who must pass the baton on to others. The lack of churches that plant churches in the twenty-first century should bother all believers.
>
> **—Conrad Mbewe, "The Joys of Planting a Church"**

2.

What are the phases of the maturation of a biblical local church from its inception to its reproduction? Chart them on the timeline in Figure 13.1. Then in a separate document, create a timeline of your own design. Research the typical time frames for completing each phase in a country or cultural context of your choosing and include those durations. You might gather this information from missionary reports, by interviewing missions agency leadership, or by interviewing missionaries who serve or have served in that context.

Figure 13.1

inception   reproduction

3.

Study rapidly reproducing church-planting and leadership-development movements in India or the Middle East, like the **disciple making movement (DMM)**, which report significant daily increases. Complete the following tasks:

a. Compare the effects of rapid-growth strategies in your chosen location to the traditional church plants that do not report dynamic daily growth. (You can learn about traditional church plants by contacting missions agencies or reading missionary newsletters.)

b. Choose one of the rapid-growth or leadership-development movements as a case study. Based on what you've learned in this lesson, how effective do you believe the movement will be for the following ministry tasks? Rate each task on a scale of 1 to 5, with 5 being "highly effective" and 1 being "very ineffective." (Recognize that your observations about the methods are preliminary and might not be correct.)

___ Raising up indigenous men to preach and teach from the Bible
___ Installing local men as elders
___ Teaching and conducting believer's baptism
___ Training local members to evangelize
___ Discipling by applying Scripture in church classes, study groups, and individually

Application Projects

1. On a separate sheet of paper, create a list of at least three core values and accompanying Scripture references that you might use to plant a new church in any context. Compare your list and your verses to the core value statements of three international church-planting organizations. What differences do you notice, if any? The following table template might be a helpful way to arrange the information.

Biblical Core Values	Organization #1: _____	Organization #2: _____	Organization #3: _____
Value #1:	Value:	Value:	Value:
Supporting Verses:	Supporting Verses:	Supporting Verses:	Supporting Verses:
	Similarities and/or differences with Value #1:	Similarities and/or differences with Value #1:	Similarities and/or differences with Value #1:

2. Use a foreign country map to locate a region, city, cluster of villages, or neighborhood that is ideal for evangelism, outreach, street preaching, or long-term church planting. To determine locations, conduct research with a team (actual, potential, or hypothetical). Then form a monthly or weekly strategy of how you would conduct ministry on that site over a two-year period. Summarize your strategy in a separate document with reference to (or images of) your map. Prepare as if to explain it before supporting church elders or a missions leadership team.

3. How does a missionary prepare his church plant for a transition to trained national leadership? Consider a specific country or cultural context as you do the following:
   a. List a series of personal questions that can help a missionary practically and spiritually think through such a transition process.

   b. Draft a few topics he might preach and teach to the congregation as part of that preparation.

   c. Suggest other discussions, activities, and events that might aid in the transition.

Leading Well

Biblical Objectives for the Planted Church

Textbook Content

CHAPTER 36: Unity in Holiness: A Biblical Theology of Race and the Church, by David Beakley

    INSERT 36.1: Sanctification: Essential for the Integrity of the Missionary's Witness, by Mark Tatlock

    INSERT 36.2: The Deconversion Stories That Go Unnoticed, by Brooks Buser

CHAPTER 37: Resolving Conflict in Cross-Cultural Settings, by Brian Biedebach

    INSERT 37.1: Impacts of the Shame-Honor Culture on the Local Church: A Case Study from the Philippines, by Sean Ransom

    INSERT 37.2: When a Plurality of Elders Is Countercultural, by Justin Cho

CHAPTER 38: Women's Ministries in Cross-Cultural Settings, by Betty Price

    INSERT 38.1: Should We Send Single Female Missionaries to the Field? by Lisa LaGeorge

CHAPTER 39: Lessons from the Field: Wisdom for Missionary Wives, by Shelbi Cullen

Key Memory Verse

There is neither Jew nor Greek, there is neither slave nor free man, there is no male and female, for you are all one in Christ Jesus.

—GALATIANS 3:28

Additional Memory Verses

- Luke 17:3–4
- Ephesians 2:14–16
- Colossians 3:12–15
- Hebrews 12:14–15
- 1 Peter 1:15–16

Scriptures for Further Meditation

- Matthew 18:15–35; Acts 6:1–6; Ephesians 4:1–6; Philippians 4:1–3; 1 Timothy 3:11; 4:12–16; Titus 2:3–8

Summary of Textbook Content

God created humanity to reflect His relational nature, but sin corrupted our relationships and marred our witness to God's glory. Thankfully, Christ came to redeem people from every tribe and language to Himself, breaking down barriers and enabling true unity across cultures within the church. Missionaries endeavor to spread this good news globally but must do so wisely by making genuine disciples and confronting sin in the planted church. Confrontation must be gentle but firm, according to Scripture. Local churches must be faithful to God's design for male spiritual leadership while encouraging all believers, regardless of demographic background, to humbly serve according to their gifts. Every culture poses unique challenges to the church, but the power of the gospel transcends them all as believers ground their relationships in holiness, integrity, and love.

Learning Objectives

- Recognize the role of holiness in maintaining a credible witness to the world.
- Acquire principles for biblical confrontation, forgiveness, and reconciliation.
- Understand how the gospel brings unity across ethnicities within the church.
- Recognize various cultural factors that threaten biblical unity and leadership.
- Affirm appropriate avenues of ministry for women in the local church.
- Appreciate the unique challenges women face on the mission field.

> Scripture calls believers to grow in Christlike holiness so that as God's set-apart people they give credible gospel witness to the lost world. Striving for holiness should manifest not just inwardly but outwardly in real, relationship-building ways—in compassionate words and selfless actions, bridging man-made divides in dark places with the light of Christ.
>
> **—Mark Tatlock, "Sanctification"**

Recall and Reflect

1. What is the source of disunity in the world today? How did it come about? [Beakley, "Unity in Holiness"]

2. What is the prerequisite for achieving unity in society? [Beakley, "Unity in Holiness"]

3. What is the difference between "market fluency" and "worldview fluency"? Which type of fluency is necessary for effective missionary work, and why? [Buser, "The De-Conversion Stories That Go Unnoticed"]

4. Define *forgiveness* and *reconciliation*. Explain the difference between the two. [Biedebach, "Resolving Conflict in Cross-Cultural Settings"]

5. What biblical practice does Ransom state that a shame-honor culture hinders believers from obeying? [Ransom, "Impacts of the Shame-Honor Culture on the Local Church"]

6. What cultural factors in South Korea make practicing biblical eldership challenging? Why? [Cho, "When a Plurality of Elders Is Countercultural"]

7. According to Titus 2:3–5, what are the four descriptions of godly older women? [Price, "Women's Ministries in Cross-Cultural Settings"]

8. What biblical examples does Price list of women who used their gifts in service to the church? What examples did she provide from the mission field? [Price, "Women's Ministries in Cross-Cultural Settings"]

9. Name LaGeorge's three examples of single women sent to the field. What was their common legacy? [LaGeorge, "Should We Send Single Female Missionaries to the Field?"]

Analyze

1. What is the relationship between unity and holiness? Can you obtain one without the other? Why or why not?

2. God is not a respecter of persons. How does the gospel confront the world's tendencies toward racial conflict, class distinctions, and tribalism/nationalism? How does the primary identity of Christians as sojourners on earth affect any former view of cultural superiority or ethnic pride?

3. How could building relationships across ethnic, cultural, or socioeconomic lines help display the power of the gospel?

4. How does understanding the distinction between true Christianity and cultural identity help the missionary to be more successful on the mission field?

5. Why should believers seek reconciliation and not merely forgiveness? List several reasons beyond what is given in Biedebach's chapter "Resolving Conflict in Cross-Cultural Settings."

6. What are some possible motives why church leaders might fail to practice church discipline?

7. What reasoning does Paul give for his insistence upon male leadership? Why is this significant? How does this reasoning represent a timeless truth and not simply culturally bound preference?

8. What are some reasons why a pastor might be reluctant to support a women's ministry and to help equip women in the church to lead it well?

9. In what ways might a women's ministry function as a support to the pastors and elders who are leading the entire church body?

Implement

1. How do you tend to respond to believers who are different from you? What can you do to help bridge the gap that exists between you and others with whom you don't naturally get along?

2. Can you identify cliques in any ministries in which you are currently involved? Around what characteristics do such cliques tend to coalesce? What can you do to help cultivate greater unity among all the members of the congregation?

3. How would you respond to someone who criticizes you for upholding a complementarian view of gender roles in the church?

4. How can you help implement and/or support a women's ministry in your church?

5. How can you show support to a single woman with a desire for missions?

6. Evaluate your own tendencies when confrontation over sin is necessary. Do you tend to avoid confrontation altogether? Do you confront in an overly harsh way? What do you need to do to handle confrontation in a more Christlike manner?

7. Describe the process you go through when determining whether to confront someone over sin. What factors contribute to your decision? Is it driven primarily by personal offense or by the welfare of the other person? How should your motives be more aligned with Scripture?

8. How would you go about confronting a church member who was spreading slander in the church? What questions would you ask? What Scriptures would you use?

> Just as single women serve in their local church—discipling, fulfilling the commands of the New Testament, or providing support for their leaders—the Lord also uses single women to serve in cross-cultural contexts for the sake of His gospel work.
>
> **—Lisa LaGeorge, "Should We Send Single Female Missionaries to the Field?"**

9. If someone observed your recent relationships and interactions, would they see the humility, patience, and forgiveness of Jesus or something else? How might growing in those areas strengthen your gospel witness?

10. What attitudes or actions of yours might blur the picture of God's holiness and make it harder for friends, coworkers or new immigrants in your community to behold Jesus? How do you plan on overcoming these attitudes and/or actions?

Ask a Missionary

1. How have you helped to encourage and equip women for missionary work or service in the church?

2. What challenges have you faced in your ministry partnerships? What has helped you to maintain unity in your partnerships?

3. What are some threats to biblical discipleship you have faced on the mission field? How did you overcome those threats and biblically disciple believers in challenging seasons?

4. What cultural differences have you encountered that unintentionally caused offense?

5. Have you needed to engage in the process of church discipline? If so, what have you learned from that experience?

6. Husbands: What challenges has your wife faced on the mission field? How have you shepherded her through them?

7. Wives: What challenges have you faced on the mission field? How have you persevered through them?

Study the Scriptures

1. Search the Gospel of John for statements by Christ about the unity He shares with the Father and the Holy Spirit. You can begin by using a concordance or Bible software to search for the persons of the Trinity. For each passage, state an implication for the unity that fellow believers are to share.

2. Consider the conflict between Euodia and Syntyche in Philippians 4:2–3. What does Paul urge them to do? How does this text prepare you to deal righteously and biblically with others when disagreements arise?

3. Study Paul's teaching on singleness in 1 Corinthians 7. How does this text influence your view on supporting single missionaries?

4. Study the characteristics prescribed for older women in Titus 2:3–5. Why do you think these qualities are emphasized? What is the impact on the church when older women are characterized by these virtues?

> By hurrying baptism, two negative outcomes become potential realities: an individual unbeliever is given false confidence that he is made right with God, and unbelievers generally now make up part of the church membership.
>
> **—Brooks Buser, "The Deconversion Stories That Go Unnoticed"**

5. Read Acts 6:1–6 and Galatians 2:11–21. Consult a study Bible to help you grasp the details. Evaluate how conflict related to ethnic distinctions is addressed in both of these passages. What is the root of the problem, and how is it solved?

6. Study Jesus' words in John 2:23–25 and John 6:60–66. In what ways does Jesus model for us in these passages what our perspective ought to be toward missions success?

Missions Research

1. Research the impact that women have had on furthering the work of the ministry. Then complete the following tasks:

    a. Report on one New Testament example, such as Dorcas, Anna, Lydia, Priscilla, or Phoebe, and what she accomplished for the Lord.

    b. Report on one female missionary from history, such as Amy Carmichael, Lilias Trotter, Elisabeth Elliot, or another woman with a written biography, and what she accomplished on the field.

    c. Fill in the following table for your personal encouragement and to consider how you might help women in a context of your choosing follow these examples.

	New Testament Woman: _____	Female Missionary: _____
Activities and Accomplishments		
Personal Encouragement		
Contextual Ministry Application		

2. Choose a country and study its immigration patterns and ethno-linguistic demographics to accomplish the following tasks:

   a. List in detail the ethnic and linguistic makeup of a particular major city, towns around the major city, and villages or rural areas farther out.

   b. Describe the ethnic and linguistic makeup of the local churches in these locations. (You might need to consult missionaries or local church leaders for this prompt.)

   c. Report what, if any, activities in the local churches reflect the ethnic diversity of their congregations, and explain how the churches seek the spiritual unity of those who are culturally diverse.

3. Read about and summarize three stories of multiethnic unity and biblical reconciliation in planted churches of missionaries from the modern era of missions onward. As a starting point, consult missionary biographies.

Application Projects

1. Identify a foreigner in your current local church context. Ask them what their experience is like and what their greatest challenges are (e.g., learning the language, understanding the culture, fitting in). Ask them how you can be a greater encouragement to them. Record your experience.

> Whether it is ethnicity, wealth, age, education, class, or politics, missionaries and elders must be on guard to shepherd the people to grow biblically according to God's program for unity among His people.
>
> **—David Beakley, "Unity in Holiness"**

2. Choose a chapter in one of the four gospels in which Jesus interacts with foreigners. (For passages, see the chapter by Tatlock, "A Messiah for All Peoples: Christ's Affirmation of a Nonexclusive Gospel.") Take the following steps:

a. Observe carefully and meditate deeply on what you learn about the character of Christ in that chapter toward others. Journal your thoughts on a separate sheet of paper (or in your personal prayer journal).

b. Identify and write down specific areas of your life in which you can better reflect Christ's heart toward people of other cultures. Confess any sin that has been exposed, and ask someone to hold you accountable to grow in that area.

c. Write down specific ways that a greater reflection of Christ in your character would directly enhance your cross-cultural witness of the gospel.

The Primary Objective

Equipping Indigenous Leaders

Textbook Content

CHAPTER 40: Indigenous Missions in Scripture and in Practice, by Paul Washer

> **INSERT 40.1:** How Can Mission Churches Be Self-Supporting? by William D. Barrick
>
> **INSERT 40.2:** Brazilians Sending Brazilians, by Jenuan Lira
>
> **INSERT 40.3:** Equipping Laypeople for Service in the South African Church, by Mark Christopher
>
> **INSERT 40.4:** A Testimony of Biblical Counseling in Latin America, by Juan Moncayo

CHAPTER 41: Removing the Scaffolding: The Missionary's Final Phase of Church Planting, by Rodney Andersen

> **INSERT 41.1:** Successful Missionary Transitions: Two Examples, by Luis Contreras
>
> **INSERT 41.2:** Gauging Successful Church-Based Training in a Minority Faith European Context, by Kristian Brackett

Key Memory Verse

And the things which you have heard from me in the presence of many witnesses, entrust these to faithful men who will be able to teach others also.

—2 TIMOTHY 2:2

Additional Memory Verses

- Ezra 7:10
- Matthew 16:18
- Acts 14:23
- 2 Timothy 1:14
- 1 Peter 4:10–11

Scriptures for Further Meditation

- Romans 15:14; Ephesians 4:7; Colossians 1:28–29; 2 Timothy 2:1–6, 15; 1 Peter 5:1–4

Summary of Textbook Content

The goal of a missionary in a foreign context should be to establish self-governing, self-supporting, and self-propagating churches that are led by indigenous leaders. This process may take time as potential leaders must be biblically qualified and adequately trained. It also takes time for congregations to grow numerically and spiritually in order to sustain a local church without outside help. Much patience and commitment is required to follow the biblical pattern set forth by the apostle Paul, but the blessed result is healthy churches that last well beyond the missionary's departure.

Learning Objectives

- Recognize the temporary role of the missionary in establishing self-governing churches.
- Understand the importance of raising up indigenous leaders.
- Identify the biblical approach to training and equipping leaders.
- Identify ways to create a self-supporting church.
- Develop strategies for successfully transitioning to local leadership and exiting the ministry.
- Develop an **indigenous missions** model after biblical examples like the apostle Paul.

> Indigenous missions . . . is really the eventual and ultimate goal of the Great Commission, and it is assumed in Jesus' command to make disciples.
>
> **—Paul Washer, "Indigenous Missions in Scripture and in Practice"**

Recall and Reflect

1. Explain the difference between cross-cultural missions and indigenous missions. [Washer, "Indigenous Missions in Scripture and in Practice"]

2. What are three lessons that can be learned from Scripture about churches sending their best missionaries? [Washer, "Indigenous Missions in Scripture and in Practice"]

3. Why does the Great Commission require sending faithful people to dwell among one another? How does Christ's incarnation serve as an example? [Washer, "Indigenous Missions in Scripture and in Practice"]

4. What are the guidelines of the "three-self" formula for indigenous missions? Define and describe each in your own words. [Barrick, "How Can Mission Churches Be Self-Supporting?"; Andersen, "Removing the Scaffolding"]

5. Which New Testament passage is particularly helpful for communicating a biblical vision of what the church ought to be at a lay level? [Christopher, "Equipping Laypeople for Service in the South African Church"]

6. According to Andersen, what should the missionary's plan be from the first day of ministry? [Andersen, "Removing the Scaffolding"]

> Faithful training ministries produce men who are teachable and who
> are on a lifelong trajectory of growth and maturity.
>
> **—Kristian Brackett, "Gauging Successful Church-Based Training in a Minority Faith European Context"**

7. What are the three conditions that Andersen advises for structuring a ministry and allowing it to grow within a church? [Andersen, "Removing the Scaffolding]

8. What does Andersen claim is needed for missionaries to step away from the decision-making process in a local church? [Andersen, "Removing the Scaffolding"]

9. Compared to the common method of using numerical metrics (conversions, programs, training enrollment, degrees awarded), what are three "more accurate measures of success" that ensure that cross-cultural, church-based training fits God's kingdom program? [Brackett, "Gauging Successful Church-Based Training in a Minority Faith European Context"]

Analyze

1. If foreign missionaries are already experienced and able to run churches, why spend the time training nationals?

2. Why is it essential for an elder or a missionary candidate to "first be tested" (1 Tim 3:10)?

3. How does **biblical counseling** function as a foundational part of the Great Commission?

4. What are some of the challenges missionaries face when they consider transitioning to new leadership?

5. What do church planters mean when they say their objective is to "work themselves out of a job"? What do you think is the basis for such a view?

6. In what ways do pastors who want to "do it all" fail to fulfill the biblical vision for the local church? How is such an attitude contradictory to the God-ordained calling of a pastor?

7. Why should missionaries resist the urge to rely on outside help to continue funding the churches they plant? What are the consequences when a church remains dependent on outside support?

8. What does a lack of giving in the local church indicate about its members? On what topics might a pastor preach to encourage his congregation to support the church's missionary efforts?

Implement

1. What are you doing to cultivate future leaders in the ministry in which you are currently involved? What might prevent you from maintaining that focus?

2. If you are working in a foreign context, how do you plan on raising up indigenous leaders in your area? Be specific.

3. Paul Washer writes, "If ministry is spiritual warfare, then the ministry that plants other ministries must be expected to be warfare of greater intensity." As a believer, how do you prepare yourself for spiritual warfare? In what ways should a missionary ready himself for "greater intensity"?

4. Pastors/elders: Is your church operating as fully self-supported? If not, what are practical steps you can take to begin transitioning to that state?

5. How can your church harness its natural assets to help offset financial costs?

6. What are some of the challenges in identifying indigenous leaders to take over the church or ministry you are leading?

7. If the Lord calls you to the mission field, would you be prepared to be a bivocational missionary if your context required it? How can you be preparing for that possibility even now?

Ask a Missionary

1. How can you tell if it's time to finally step out of ministry to pass on leadership to a local leader? What are some of the challenges to reaching that point?

2. How long did it take you to raise up indigenous leaders in your location?

> Our participation in Jesus' Great Commission is no longer only a desire; it is a blessed reality, founded on biblical convictions and providential partnerships. Our experience has convinced us that the Lord can do the same in any place where His people decide to obey.
>
> **—Jenuan Lira, "Brazilians Sending Brazilians"**

3. If you had to support yourself bivocationally, how did you structure your time? What advice would you give to a missionary who must also be bivocational?

4. What was the transition like from academia to full-time ministry? What advice would you give to the graduate preparing for the mission field?

Study the Scriptures

1. Study Paul's farewell address to the Ephesian elders in Acts 20:17–38. What does this passage teach us regarding Paul's approach to training local church leaders? What principles and priorities should the missionary keep in mind as he seeks to train up and transition to indigenous leadership?

2. How does Acts 14:21–23 model a process for establishing indigenous churches and raising up indigenous leaders? Outline the practical steps contained there.

3. Read 2 Thessalonians 3:6–15. Why does Paul speak so harshly of those who are unwilling to work? What does such an attitude communicate about how one views others in the local church? How does this relate to a church's responsibility to be self-supporting and care for those in legitimate need?

4. Study 2 Corinthians 9:6–15. What attitudes toward giving are taught in this passage? How does this indicate that a church should labor to provide for the needs of its own congregation besides others?

5. Study 2 Corinthians 6:7; 10:4–6; Ephesians. 6:10–18. How do these passages describe, in Washer's words, "the scriptural weapons of warfare"?

Missions Research

1. Research how the particular problems of the worldview of your culture (actual or potential) might require specific attention when providing biblical counseling for such issues as Christian marriages in difficulty, church leaders in conflict, parenting challenges, premarital relationships, or besetting sins. Write out your conclusions (focusing on the worldview) for several of these problems and their biblical antidote with the Scriptures you would use in a counseling context.

2. Find a church plant in two different foreign fields led by faithful missionaries who are supported by your local church (or if necessary, by a local church in your network). Research the history of missions in those foreign fields and answer the following questions:
   a. How challenging was it for the early foreign missionaries to transition leadership in the local churches to indigenous elders? Support your conclusion with a specific historical case.

   b. How prevalent are biblically sound local churches with indigenous leadership today? What do your findings suggest about the missionary transition process in the local churches there generally?

   c. Compare your findings between the two regions and suggest what cultural and pastoral factors might be behind the successes or failures.

Application Projects

1. Speak with your church leader(s) about opportunities for members to serve as biblical counselors. Discuss how formal training in biblical counseling could benefit your church. Research the training and accountability required in a program, such as the Association of Certified Biblical Counselors (ACBC) or Overseas Instruction in Counseling (OIC). In a separate document list the benefits you discussed, draft a potential timeline that you or someone in your local church might follow to become certified in programs like ACBC or OIC, and describe how it might be coordinated with other missions training.

2. On a separate sheet of paper, compile a list of Scripture passages that instruct local churches on the practice of giving. Based on these texts, summarize the biblical theology of giving in the space below. What motivates giving? What are its objectives? What is the manner in which giving should be done? Finally, create a teaching outline that you could potentially use in the future to inform a church congregation on why and how they ought to give biblically.

3. Work with a team to outline a potential nine-month training program for your local church to equip and support indigenous missionaries. Include training or teaching topics, biblical texts to study, theological resources to read, and opportunities for skills development. Fill out the following template, possibly adding other columns on a separate sheet of paper, such as logistics to consider and challenges. Consider asking an elder of your church to give you feedback on your design.

Month	Topics	Texts	Resources	Opportunities
1				
2				
3				
4				
5				
6				
7				
8				
9				

Equipping Leaders through Theological Education

Textbook Content

CHAPTER 42: The First Seminary: A Biblical Case for Pastoral Training, by Nathan Busenitz

> **INSERT 42.1:** Intentional Discipleship in Lebanon, by Maurice Boutros and Mark Jeffries

CHAPTER 43: Training Pastors Theologically: A *Sine Qua Non* of Biblical Missions, by Brad Klassen

> **INSERT 43.1:** The Legacy of Pastoral Training in South Africa: A Case Study from the Limpopo Region, by David Beakley and Charlie Rampfumedzi
>
> **INSERT 43.2:** Training Preachers in East Asia, by Jimmy Tan

CHAPTER 44: Drafting the Distinctives of a Philosophy of Global Theological Education, by Rubén Videira-Soengas

CHAPTER 45: Foundation Blocks for Faithful Pastoral Training, by Marco Bartholomae

> **INSERT 45.1:** How to Be a Paul to Your National Timothy, by Todd Dick
>
> **INSERT 45.2:** Theological Education, Worldview, and the Church's Mission: A Case Study from Kitwe, Zambia, by Philip S. Hunt, Billy C. Sichone, and Benjamin Straub

Key Memory Verse

Brothers, join in following my example, and look for those who walk according to the pattern you have in us.

—PHILIPPIANS 3:17

Additional Memory Verses

- Luke 6:40
- 1 Corinthians 11:1

- Ephesians 4:20–24
- 1 Thessalonians 2:7–12
- 2 Peter 3:18

Scriptures for Further Meditation

- Acts 19:8–10; 1 Corinthians 9:22; Ephesians 4:11–14; 1 Timothy 3:15; 4:13; 2 Timothy 2:15; 2 Peter 3:18

Summary of Textbook Content

Throughout the centuries, faithful men have engaged in a global effort to pass the baton of sound biblical truth to the next generation. From Ephesus to Zambia, faithful men have labored to "teach others also," united by a love for God and an undying belief in the power of His Word. Out of this bedrock grows the mandate to teach—to impart truth in ways that change hearts and minds. Yet theological instruction is empty if not delivered by individuals whose lives have been transformed by the truth they proclaim. Thus, personal discipleship must accompany formal instruction. As students develop both theological clarity and godly character, they are then equipped to serve and strengthen the local church, which is the true biblical aim of all theological **education**.

Learning Objectives

- Understand the biblical basis for training pastors and church leaders.
- Embrace strengthening the local church as the true aim of theological education.
- Acknowledge the need to balance formal instruction with personal discipleship.
- Understand ways in which theological education can be culturally appropriate to local churches within their own context.
- Know the necessity of shaping students' worldviews biblically.
- Embrace the mandate to disciple the next generation.

> The mandate of disciple-making requires the explicit act of comprehensive instruction that aims toward wholesale obedience.
>
> —Brad Klassen, "Training Pastors Theologically: A *Sine Qua Non* of Biblical Missions"

Recall and Reflect

1. What was the first seminary that we know of in history? [Busenitz, "The First Seminary"]

2. Explain the three consequences of neglecting pastoral training that Klassen identifies. [Klassen, "Training Pastors Theologically"]

3. According to Tan, what are the three ways the church in Asia can be supported? [Tan, "Training Preachers in East Asia"]

4. What are the three distinctives that differentiate Christian education from secular education? [Videira-Soengas, "Drafting the Distinctives of a Philosophy of Global Theological Education"]

5. What are the four questions that must be asked to ensure a theological program accomplishes its objectives? [Videira-Soengas, "Drafting the Distinctives of a Philosophy of Global Theological Education"]

6. What are the five core biblical values that trainers of indigenous leaders must impart to their students? [Bartholomae, "Foundational Blocks for Faithful Pastoral Training"]

7. What are the four primary blocks to sustain a training center? [Bartholomae, "Foundational Blocks for Faithful Pastoral Training"]

8. What are the characteristics that should be present in a training center's director, as well as its advisory board members? [Bartholomae, "Foundational Blocks for Faithful Pastoral Training"]

9. What are the three realities in a missions context that emphasize the importance of ongoing personal discipleship? [Dick, "How to Be a Paul to Your National Timothy"]

10. What is meant by "brain drain" in the context of missions, and how does this occur? [Hunt, Sichone, and Straub, "Theological Education, Worldview, and the Church's Mission"]

Analyze

1. Explain why the training of indigenous pastors is equally important in fulfilling the Great Commission as evangelism.

2. Is theological instruction equivalent to spiritual discipleship? In what ways do they overlap? In what ways are they different? How can mentors ensure that they uphold both objectives?

3. How has theological education succeeded as a servant of local churches? How has it failed?

4. What is at stake if theological education becomes the means to an end other than knowing Christ?

5. How can historically Western theological education models do better with worldview awareness and engagement? What is at stake if education fails to engage worldviews?

6. Explain how Paul's mandate to Timothy in 2 Timothy 2:2 was modeled by Paul himself in Acts 19:8–10.

7. What are the six additional blocks that Bartholomae identifies, which are built on top of the four foundational blocks of a training center? In your own words, what do these six blocks have in common, and what is their aim and purpose? Why are the four primary blocks more foundational?

8. What opportunities and risks accompany the maintaining of local government accreditation? If an institution is already accredited, what mentality does it need to retain to ensure it remains biblically faithful?

9. What are the consequences if a formal theological institution does not take serious measures to evaluate if its participants are genuine believers?

> Theological education must actively position itself as a servant of the local churches in its own context if it is to successfully strengthen churches rather than weaken them.
>
> **—Philip Hunt, Billy Sichone, and Benjamin Straub, "Theological Education, Worldview, and the Church's Mission: A Case Study from Kitwe, Zambia"**

Implement

1. How do the consequences of neglecting pastoral training highlighted by Klassen influence your view of the importance of this task?

2. Evaluate your ministry relationships that have a training component to them, if any. To what degree do they involve theological education compared with life-on-life discipleship? What steps can you take for greater balance in training those around you practically?

3. Consider the people who have had the most influence in your life personally. Summarize the aspects of their life and character that you most want to emulate. How will you intentionally go about modeling those same qualities to others you disciple, either now or in the future?

4. Take some time to evaluate all you have learned this year in your theological pursuits. List some of the doctrinal areas in which your thinking has developed. What impact have those truths had on your living? What impact ought they to have?

5. Busenitz explains that Paul's faithfulness to Christ's imperative and His sacrificial investment are the factors that led to widespread impact. How might you need to adjust your priorities for training others to have a greater impact for Christ in light of this pattern?

Ask a Missionary

1. Summarize your strategy for training indigenous leaders for the work of the ministry.

2. What kind of theological education is available in your context for men who desire **formal education**? Do you advise them to pursue these options?

3. What are the most common areas in which the indigenous disciples you serve need the most discipleship?

4. What are some subject areas of formal training programs that might help address the most pressing concerns in the local churches of your context? What are some elective courses you would like these programs to include?

5. Who has had a significant impact on you spiritually? What have you learned from them, and how do you want to follow their example in your Christian walk and in how you disciple younger believers?

Study the Scriptures

1. Explain the connection between Christ's mandate in Matthew 28:18–20 and Paul's mandate in 2 Timothy 2:2? How does this affect your understanding of the Great Commission and how we go about accomplishing it?

> If Christians are disciples of Christ, always learning to obey Him, then theological education, whether formal or informal, is a necessity for all men and women in the local church.
>
> —Rubén Videira-Soengas, "Drafting the Distinctives of a Philosophy of Global Theological Education"

2. Study Paul's instructions in Titus 1:5–9. How does the appointment of well-trained and biblically qualified elders relate to the fulfillment of the Great Commission? How might progress in the Great Commission be thwarted if diligence here is not pursued?

3. Study Paul's model of spiritual leadership in 1 Thessalonians 2:1–12. Consider the balance Paul provides in this passage between proclamation of the truth and life example. What does it mean to impart "not only the gospel of God but also our own lives"? How do you think it connects with Paul's description of himself as a spiritual parent? Is there anyone in whom you are investing this way?

4. Revisit the connection between Paul's leadership training efforts in Acts 19:8–10 and his instruction to Timothy in 2 Timothy 2:2. Read two commentaries on each passage. How does the connection affect your view of the doctrinal and missional legacy we inherit from Paul and the rest of the apostles?

5. Study 1 Corinthians 3:10–15. What does it mean to "be careful how [one] builds" on the foundation Paul laid? What are some ways that people can build on the foundation wrongly? What does quality work look like, and how does one go about accomplishing it?

Missions Research

1. Read about the history of five prominent evangelical theological institutions (college, university, seminary, graduate programs) in your home country or a country of your choosing. Then write an essay to do the following:
   a. Provide a survey that briefly summarizes the role of pastor-theologians in the founding and original goals of the schools. For many schools such information can be found on their websites, while for others historical dictionaries or accounts need to be searched.
   b. Choose one institution from your list as a case study, and analyze if there has been a pattern of biblical fidelity, drift away from, or even resurgence toward theologically conservative **evangelicalism** since its founding. Explain with historical detail the influences behind the movement or fidelity, and state how one might characterize the school's current doctrinal commitments and philosophy of education. You might refer to the school's website and/or academic catalog for a list of its learning objectives and goals.

2. What does it look like in your cultural context to receive "pastoral training"? Find a seminary or Bible school near you that awards ministry degrees. Research and then summarize what student discipleship and ministry practicums the programs require and what partnerships they promote with local pastors. What is such a student trained to actually do? How does this training relate to the pastoral and preaching responsibilities described in the New Testament?

3. Choose a missionary from the Reformation era forward who was trained in a theological institution for ministry and who then faithfully established or served in theological training on the field (formal or informal). Create a brief presentation that you could share with a church or school class, bringing together the principles of this lesson with the biographical sketch of your chosen missionary.

Application Projects

1. Work with your team (actual or potential) to design pastoral training goals and steps toward achieving them by doing the following:
   a. Each teammate should list individually what they believe to be the top five goals of pastoral training and rank them in order of importance.

   b. Each teammate should list the top five impediments to training men for pastoral leadership in their country or cultural context.

   c. Discuss the teammates' lists of goals and impediments together to expand, reword, refine, and re-rank them as a composite list in a separate document.
   d. Discuss and record in that document practical, actionable steps that can be taken in and through local churches to achieve each goal and to confront and overcome each impediment.
   e. Bring the team's draft of goals, impediments, and steps to a select group of trusted local church leaders for feedback, and then as a team discuss it and pray. Summarize the results.

2. Preferably with a team, go through the early stages of developing a certificate-level program for a local church that trains men and women (from teenagers upward) in Bible and theology. Take the following steps in a separate document:

a. Identify a potential vision for the program.

b. State the program's overall objectives and main target group.

c. List the general content, skills, and qualities you seek to impart.

d. State which core courses will be needed to achieve the vision for the program.

e. Draft the overall student learning outcomes that will be measured.

3. Consider the Education Process diagram in Figure 16.1. Once you've understood the diagram, map the certificate-level program that you developed earlier onto this diagram. In the space surrounding it, write out brief answers to the questions in bulleted lists next to each question. Use a separate sheet of paper if necessary.

Figure 16.1

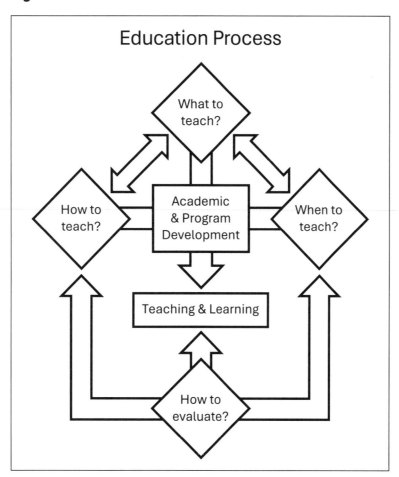

4. Students in formal theological training can sometimes become spiritually stagnant. Choose one such program in your country and cultural context, and propose at least five practical methods—such as assigning students application projects—to ensure the students' continuing spiritual health. Focus on strategies and processes for helping all students develop a consistent pattern of self-reflection and teachability that will lead to spiritual growth in their walks with the Lord.

5. Choose a location foreign to you where the believers express (actually or hypothetically) a desire to form a pastoral training center. Then use figures 16.2 and 16.3 to do the following:

a. Identify a sequence that can be reasonably followed to progress toward forming a pastoral training center at your chosen location. Number the blocks in sequence from 1 to 10. Are any foundation blocks on site already operative?

Figure 16.2

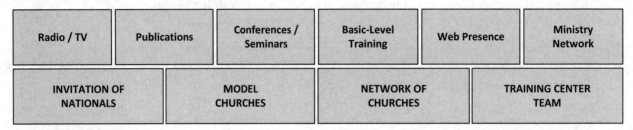

Figure 16.3

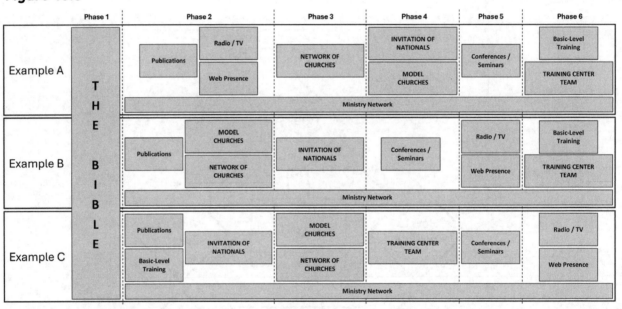

b. Note the variety of examples in Figure 16.3 for developing a training center. Does your design align more with example A, B, C, or something else? Circle the label of the design most aligned with yours. Then on a separate sheet of paper, sketch your own sequence diagram and explain your rationale.

c. What role could you see yourself fulfilling at such a training center, whether in administration, teaching, or support?

Equipping Leaders through Musical Instruction

Textbook Content

CHAPTER 46: Embracing Theologically Sound Music in a Theologically Unsound World, by Scott N. Callaham

> **INSERT 46.1:** The Role of the Arts in Evangelism, by Paul T. Plew
>
> **INSERT 46.2:** Music Ministry to Families in France, by Philippe Viguier

CHAPTER 47: Teaching Music in the Global Church, by Thomas Hochstetter and Kellie Cunningham

> **INSERT 47.1:** Music Education as Discipleship in Uganda, by Kellie Cunningham

Key Memory Verse

Let the word of Christ dwell in you richly, with all wisdom teaching and admonishing one another with psalms and hymns and spiritual songs, singing with gratefulness in your hearts to God.

—COLOSSIANS 3:16

Additional Memory Verses

- Psalm 96:1–2
- Psalm 98:1
- John 4:23–24
- Ephesians 5:19–20
- James 5:13

Scriptures for Further Meditation

- 1 Chronicles 16:9; Psalms 30:4; 67:3–4; 105:1–2; 149:1; Acts 16:25; Revelation 5:9

Summary of Textbook Content

Music plays an indispensable role in the spiritual health of the local church. It is an act of worship to God, a form of ministry to the saints, a means of guarding the flock against error, a tool for proclaiming the gospel to the lost, and a mandate prescribed by God in His Word. Because of the influence that music has on its hearers, church leaders must exercise discernment in both the selection of songs that their congregations will sing, as well as the training of those who will lead the local church in worship through music.

Learning Objectives

- Understand the purpose of music in the local church.
- Identify common cultural pitfalls in musical worship.
- Recognize the biblical qualifications of worship leaders.
- Embrace the use of music to equip believers both young and old.
- Consider how to use music evangelistically.
- Gain biblical principles for worship song selection.

> Music is a powerful means of rehearsing the doctrines of the nature and works of God, confessing one's faith in them, exalting Christ as head of the church, and even using these truths to evangelize the listening unbeliever.
>
> **—Kellie Cunningham, "Music Education as Discipleship in Uganda"**

Recall and Reflect

1. Define and contrast the normative principle and the regulative principle of worship. [Callaham, "Embracing Theologically Sound Music in a Theologically Unsound World"]

2. What are the two derivatives based on the "regulative principle" approach to music? [Callaham, "Embracing Theologically Sound Music in a Theologically Unsound World"]

3. What two factors does Callaham argue must be considered when evaluating the theology of worship music? [Callaham, "Embracing Theologically Sound Music in a Theologically Unsound World"]

4. From where do art and beauty come? What Scripture passages provide the answer? [Plew, "The Role of the Arts in Evangelism"]

5. What is the most effective way to identify qualified music leaders? [Hochstetter and Cunningham, "Teaching Music in the Global Church"]

6. What are some of the benefits of family worship? [Hochstetter and Cunningham, "Teaching Music in the Global Church"]

7. How does music equip believers with the Word of Christ for life's daily spiritual battles? [Hochstetter and Cunningham, "Teaching Music in the Global Church"]

> Worship leaders have the responsibility of equipping musicians to strive for excellence as they serve the Lord with their art. In so doing, they help produce lifelong worshipers in their churches.
>
> —Thomas Hochstetter and Kellie Cunningham, "Teaching Music in the Global Church"

8. What does the term **ethnodoxology** mean? [Hochstetter and Cunningham, "Teaching Music"]

9. What were Bosco Adama's three goals for accomplishing discipleship through music, and what steps did he take to accomplish those goals? [Cunningham, "Music Education as Discipleship in Uganda"]

Analyze

1. How does the fact that Scripture is not just the final or primary authority, but the sole authority, affect your approach toward worship in the church?

2. Why is it essential that Christians worship through music "in spirit and truth" (John 4:24)? What problems would arise if one of these two components were missing?

3. What are some specific ways that emotional expressiveness in leading worship could manipulate the emotions of the congregation? How might a lack of expression in the music leader hamper the worshipful expression of the congregants?

4. What is the danger of vagueness and ambiguity in lyrics? How might the choice of lyrics enhance or compromise the edification of the saints?

5. Why is it important to evaluate not just the theology of song lyrics but the theology of the songwriter as well? What are the risks of neglecting this aspect?

6. What is the connection between the gift of exhortation and the process of writing songs and leading music in the local church?

7. What are some ways that churches can come alongside parents to train children "in the nurture and admonition of the Lord" (Eph 6:4 KJV) through music?

8. Viguier states that the combination of music and children is a powerful tool to bring the gospel into people's homes. How might children's music be used to extend the gospel to other family members?

9. Why is it important that the selection of evangelistic music, from lyrics to style, consider the following circumstances: the cultural context, the nature of the music event itself, and the attendant sermon topic?

10. What are some ways that a local church pastor's expository preaching in an event like a Sunday church service might become less effective if his sermons are coupled with theologically compromised music?

Implement

1. What principles do you follow to evaluate the theological quality of the songs you listen to today?

2. If a member of the church requested to sing a song congregationally that was not doctrinally sound, how would you counsel that person regarding the purpose of music in the church?

3. If a church leader is concerned that the music team is not consistently leading the congregation in biblical worship, perhaps due to song choices or to the design of the service, what are some first steps he should take to address what he perceives to be the problem? List at least three initial steps.

4. How would you prepare a new music leader in your church for effective ministry? What objectives would you set for him?

5. What are ways that a local church can provide opportunities for those who are musically talented to exercise their gifting? Be specific.

6. What are some ways in which you can reach people with the gospel through music?

7. Which Scriptures would you include in the description of a music ministry for a local church website? Which biblical principles would you draw from those verses?

Ask a Missionary

1. Have you encountered any unbiblical principles or doctrinal errors in the music of the people you serve? How have you shepherded them toward a more theologically sound understanding of music?

2. When it comes to the ministry of music, how do you distinguish between what is merely a cultural preference versus what is an unbiblical expression of worship?

3. What steps did you take to identify theologically sound songs in the language of the people you serve?

4. Have you found it more effective to translate existing hymns/worship songs into a native language or to compose new songs in that language?

5. How has musical expression/worship differed in your missionary context from your previous exposure? How have you adapted to a new environment?

6. How have you observed art serving as a platform to promote Christianity as well as false religion in your missionary context?

Study the Scriptures

1. Ephesians 5:19 and Colossians 3:16 are two of the most foundational verses for understanding the role of music in the church. Study the passages in which these verses appear. How do the teachings of these passages influence your understanding of the purpose of music in the church?

> Whether performing with evangelistic purposes or writing biblically sound poetry that moves the mind and spirit, art forms provide persuasive vehicles to gather an audience and share the truth of Christ in His beauty.
>
> **—Paul T. Plew, "The Role of the Arts in Evangelism"**

2. When defining the role of music in the church, Hochstetter and Cunningham list several scriptural examples of music as a component of worship. Look up the passages in that paragraph, and in your own words list what principles for worship can be derived from each of them.

3. Read Psalm 105, and then return to study verses 1–7. Read a devotional commentary or two on this first stanza. According to these verses, what should be our priorities in worship? How does this psalm influence the way you think about biblically rich worship lyrics?

4. Recall your previous study of Psalm 67 (lesson 8) and reread the psalm. How does it inform your understanding of the relationship between missions and music?

5. Review the qualifications for deacons listed in 1 Timothy 3:8–12. Why would these qualifications be necessary for an individual who serves as a music leader?

Missions Research

1. In your country or cultural context, or in one similar to yours, look for events such as concerts, conferences, camp retreats, Christian schools, and so on to identify the worship songs believers sing most regularly. Then do the following:
   a. Analyze three of the most popular (repeated) worship songs for how these songs satisfy biblical principles of worship. List them below.

   b. Conduct research on the songwriters and evaluate what theological positions they appear to hold. You might check if their songs are most used by certain denominations or church networks versus others (e.g., Assemblies of God, Brethren, international, nondenominational). List the songwriters and their distinctives below.

c. For each of the songs, state the reasons you would or would not recommend singing them in a potential church plant in that country or cultural context.

2. List five of the top sinful beliefs, expressions, or practices you are concerned might most readily syncretize (blend) with Christian music and worship from your current cultural context or potential culture of service. Describe the items in detail, then suggest at least two preventive measures a missionary or a local church leader should take to mitigate the risk of syncretism in music and worship practices.

3. Look up the websites or social media accounts of five of the largest local churches in a country of interest. Answer the following questions based on your observations:

   a. What does the typical structuring of their Sunday service suggest about the importance of music in worship? Roughly what percentage of the service is dedicated on average to music, to preaching, and to announcements/greetings?

> Music opens doors to hearts, and children open doors to families. The combination of music and children is a powerful tool to bring the gospel into people's homes.
>
> **—Philippe Viguier, "Music Ministry to Families in France"**

   b. Is much attention drawn to musical performance in the visual media the accounts use to promote their church (e.g., photos, video clips, sound bites)? How prominent is the musical component in their media compared to other aspects of the church, such as preaching and teaching, discipleship, evangelism, and so on?

   c. How do they express the role of music when they speak or write about their church?

   d. Based on these observations, what appear to be the priorities/commitments of the church?

e. How do the churches compare/contrast with each other? Consider creating a table or chart on a separate sheet of paper to synthesize your findings across the five churches.

Application Projects

1. Briefly interview indigenous music and worship leaders in several local churches across denominations in your cultural context or one of your choosing. Ask them the following questions and record their answers on a separate sheet of paper:
   a. Is there a need to compose music and lyrics for use in the local churches here? If so, why?
   b. What is your weekly process for selecting worship songs for the congregation and for the church's musicians (choirs, ensembles, soloists, etc.)?
   c. What is your church's process for evaluating and introducing new songs to the worship repertoire?
   d. How do you disciple believers in the music ministry you lead?
   e. What are three ways missionaries and church leaders can encourage musically talented believers to edify the body through music?

2. In a separate document create a one- to two-year training plan for raising up a music leader or co-leader in your local church.
   a. Identify the objectives for the person.
   b. Detail the minimum required qualifications to serve (e.g., musical skill, character, doctrine).
   c. Outline a process aimed at achieving those objectives, including songwriting training, additional music lessons, early opportunities for performance or leading, and active discipleship and Bible training.

3. In a separate document create a philosophy of ministry statement for the music ministry at a new church plant. Consider the relationship of the music ministry to the other ministries of the church, such as preaching, teaching, discipling, and evangelizing.

Recommendations for missionaries to incorporate musical art into their ministry:

1. Sing songs in the language of the country you are in.
2. Have someone on your team who speaks the language of the people.
3. Perform familiar songs from the country by renowned composers.
4. Sing lyrics that come directly from Scripture.
5. Choose appropriate music that is of the highest possible quality.
6. Learn the national anthem of the country you are in.
7. Be friendly, kind, encouraging, affirming, and joyous.
8. Be Christlike.

The following list contains timeless principles for writing new hymns and songs of faith, drawn from the Psalms and from the rich hymnody of the Reformation.

- Make congregational singing your goal.
- Use a content-first approach that aims to expound biblical truths.
- Write songs that aren't restricted to being performed in a specific musical context (e.g., a praise band or a choir).
- Create melodies that can easily be sung by a variety of people.
- Write in the style of your cultural context in your generation, unless doing so would be **syncretistic**.
- Write for a variety of occasions (e.g., praising God, crying for help, thanking God, reminding one another about God's character and works)
- Utilize different musical sounds to match tone to words (e.g., joy, sadness, meditation, triumph).
- Be creative and work hard to write excellent and memorable poetry that will honor God.

Equipping Leaders through Print Resources

Textbook Content

Key Memory Verse

Finally, brothers, pray for us that the word of the Lord will spread rapidly and be glorified, just as it did also with you.

—2 THESSALONIANS 3:1

Additional Memory Verses

- Joshua 1:8
- Psalm 19:7–11
- Nehemiah 8:8
- Acts 17:11
- 1 Timothy 4:13

Scriptures for Further Meditation

- Psalm 119:18; Romans 15:4; 1 Corinthians 2:7–16; 1 Thessalonians 5:27; 1 Timothy 4:16; 2 Peter 1:3–4

Summary of Textbook Content

If biblical missions involves planting new churches and those churches are supposed to function as the pillar and support of the truth (1 Tim 3:15), then resourcing those churches with an accurate Bible translation and theologically sound educational material is indispensable to the accomplishment of that goal. But this is no easy task. A host of questions must be carefully considered. Who should be the translators? With whom should translators partner? What should be their priorities in translation? Which translation method will they use? How will success be measured? Which resources should be prioritized, and why? These questions and more are highly consequential and must be answered with great discernment if God's aim to extend the gospel to all tribes and tongues will be accomplished to His greatest praise and glory.

Learning Objectives

- Comprehend the biblical motivations for resourcing the global church with Bible translations and printed materials.

- Grasp the biblical basis for Bible translation and its relationship to the Great Commission.
- Evaluate the historical rationales for Bible translation.
- Understand different translation theories and their implications for accuracy and application.
- Learn to assess the translation and resourcing needs for a given cultural context.
- Consider best practices for translation management, including team development, quality control, technology utilization, and so on.
- Identify administrative skills needed for securing permissions, logistics, marketing, and other publishing tasks.

> Declaring the praises of Christ before the lost is called evangelism; before the church it is called edification; and directly to God it is called exaltation. Resourcing the global church is vital to worship, fellowship, and evangelism. Hence, it is vital to the Christian life.
>
> **—Aaron Shryock, "The Rationale for Bible Translation"**

Recall and Reflect

1. Where in Scripture do we find the first connection between language and mission? [Tatlock, "Why Bible Translation is Critical in God's Plan of Redemption"]

2. In what way has the Holy Spirit Himself established a precedent for Bible translation? [Shryock, "The Rationale for Bible Translation"]

3. Define and contrast the formal equivalence and dynamic equivalence theories of Bible translation. [Barrick, "Bible Translation"]

4. What are the two tools that Allushi says will help Albanian speakers to rightly discern God's truth? [Allushi, "Bible Translation in Albania Yesterday and Today"]

5. How does the idea of a "pastor-translator" affect the work of translation? [Davis, "Missions and the Pastor-Translator"]

6. What is the ultimate missionary resource, and how is it ultimate over other publications, tools, or skills? [Kress, "Resourcing the Global Church"]

7. How did Ezra engage in "biblical resourcing"? [Kress, "Resourcing the Global Church"]

8. What are the three different categories of learning that guide publishing efforts? [Tatlock, "Translating and Publishing for Training"]

9. According to Heaton, what are the two issues those who are involved in global publishing should think carefully about? [Heaton, "Practical Early Steps for Global Translation Publishing"]

10. What problems did Pineda Dale identify with the resources that are currently available in Spanish? What types of resources does he say are still lacking? [Pineda Dale, "Publishing for the 'Nonreading,' Spanish-Speaking, Latin American Church"]

Analyze

1. Consider Barrick's example of translating the word *love* into the Hdi language. Why is it so critical to understand the nuances of both the original language and the receptor language when engaging in translation?

2. Why are the missionary activities of evangelism, discipleship, church planting, and leadership training all dependent on a good, complete translation of God's Word?

3. Why are pastoral qualities needed for a Bible translator?

4. Explain the importance of Bible translation for guarding against false teaching.

5. What are the dangers of attempting to translate theological terms into another language? What steps can be taken to overcome those challenges faithfully?

6. What is the connection between the grammatical-historical hermeneutic and the ability to derive accurate significance and application in a new target language?

7. What are the benefits of creating a theologically sound bookstore at your local church?

8. Why should Bible translators have believers and not unbelievers in mind when translating the Bible?

> Apart from one's personal influence in the lives of others, translation and publication is arguably the most enduring ministry one could have on the mission field.
>
> **—Walter Heaton, "Practical Early Steps for Global Translation Publishing"**

9. Following Kyle Davis's suggestion that the process of Bible translation should intersect with each stage of the missionary endeavor, list some potential benefits of this intersection at each of the individual stages in the diagram below.

Figure 18.1

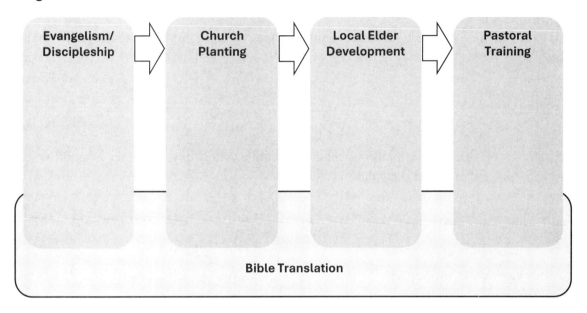

Implement

1. How would you respond to someone who said the Bible cannot be truly understood anymore because its meaning has been lost in translation?

2. Consider some of the most helpful tools you use when studying the Bible. How would your ministry efforts be impacted if you didn't possess those resources? How does this influence your understanding of the translation needs of the global church?

3. What are some ways you can begin praying for the translation and resourcing needs that many areas of the world still face?

4. Would you consider Bible translation merely a prerequisite for obeying Christ's commands or an act of obedience in and of itself? Explain your answer.

5. What practical steps can you take to better equip your local congregation with theologically sound resources?

6. Why is it important that a pastor point his congregation to a variety of good books in addition to feeding them God's Word from the pulpit?

7. How is your view of the ongoing significance of translation work influenced by the fact that much of it today is being done by widely various groups?

Ask a Missionary

1. How adequate do you consider the Bible translations in the country you serve? What problems have you encountered due to poor translation?

2. What translated resources have proven the most useful to your church congregation? What resources do you most want to be translated into the language of the people you serve?

3. What extrabiblical resources or study tools do you most desire to be translated into the language of the people you serve? Why would these resources be particularly helpful?

4. If applicable, what efforts have you made to enhance your translation skills since joining the mission field, either with the biblical text or the target language/culture you are translating to?

5. What role are you currently playing in the Bible translation efforts going on in your target language?

Study the Scriptures

1. Recall the various components of the Great Commission in Matthew 28:18–20. How would these activities be hindered without an adequate Bible translation? How would additional biblical resources further aid in the fulfillment of Jesus' mandate in this text?

2. Identify each of Paul's objectives laid out in Ephesians 4:11–16. Explain how the provision of faithful biblical resources in native languages will help churches around the world in accomplishing these objectives.

3. Study the global quality of the worship of Christ in the book of Revelation (Rev 5:9–10; 7:9–10). How does translation and publishing contribute to this outcome?

4. Read the story of Ezra instructing the people of Israel in Nehemiah 8:1–8. How does this passage fit within the context of the book of Nehemiah? What led up to this event, and what was the outcome of it? How does this story connect with the practice of translation as well as of publishing/resourcing?

> **Good books make good disciplers.**
>
> **—Newton Chilingulo, "A Lending Library and Bookstore in a Malawian Church"**

5. Read Colossians 2 and identify Paul's goals for the Colossian believers, as well as the dangers that threaten to impede those goals. How could a robust Christian library in one's own language help to achieve these goals and protect against the threats.

Missions Research

1. Choose a country or region that has a primary language you neither speak nor hear in your current cultural context. Then complete the following tasks:

 a. Research and summarize what Christian resources and Bible study tools are available in that language, including the number of Bible translation versions. Consult publishers' websites, catalogs, and any lists of materials offered or sold at conferences, camps, and seminars in that language.

 b. Do the same for other study resources, such as systematic theologies, dictionaries, concordances, commentaries, biblical counseling resources, Christian living books, audio sermons, and so on.

 c. Document the challenges you discover to supplying published resources for churches within a country that speaks your chosen language. Consider corresponding with publishers or local churches in that country to obtain current and detailed information.

2. Contact at least three missionaries serving in very different areas of the world. Ask them which translated or published resources have been most helpful for them in their ministries. Is there any overlap between the missionaries? Do their answers vary depending on the type of ministry in which they are engaged?

3. Consider Bible translations in your current linguistic context by answering the following prompts:

   a. How adequate do you believe the Bible translations are that local churches use for preaching, teaching, and discipleship?

   b. List the criteria by which you determine a translation's validity.

   c. If you believe a specific translation to be lacking in some way, provide evidence and reasons to the best of your ability from the text itself.

   d. Give an example of a potential consequence of an inadequate translation for pastors, teachers, leaders, and church members from one of the versions you considered.

4. Research one Bible translation in English or in another language group that follows a "formal equivalence" approach to translation. Also research one version that follows a "dynamic equivalence" approach. For both translations, read any material made available by the translators that explains their methods, approach, or strategy taken to produce this version. Some discussion might be found in the preface of the translation version, in online or print interviews, or through other materials. Compare and contrast the methods of both translations for interpreting and expounding the text.

5. Choose a people group of your interest, a people to whom the gospel has been carried and for whom a Bible translation has been completed. Then respond to the following two prompts:

   a. Research the order in which the following stages of the missionary endeavor were undertaken: evangelism/discipleship, church planting, local elder development, and pastoral training. Write each one in the appropriate box in Figure 18.2.

   Figure 18.2

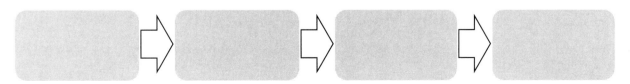

b. Draw an outer box encompassing the stages of the missionary endeavor from when the work of Bible translation began to when the translation was completed.

c. From your research, explain below how the process of Bible translation was affected by believers and/or unbelievers in the missionary's target people group.

Application Projects

1. Find a Bible translator in your country or a language group of your choosing who seems to follow conservative principles and procedures in translation work. Ask if you may sit in on at least one meeting of the translation team as a silent observer. Take notes of your observations, detailing any discussions raised or decisions made about a biblical term, concept, or local term. On a separate sheet of paper write out a brief summary of the meeting and the translation team's overall progress in their project.

2. Create a potential recommended reading list that would benefit believers in a church plant of the target language you chose earlier. Though resources might be limited, do your best to answer the following questions:

a. What general types of resources (e.g., systematic theologies, commentaries, biblical counseling resources, Christian living books) would you recommend to the following types of believers?

   i. New believers.

   ii. Believers who have come from other churches.

   iii. Future church leaders.

b. What specific titles would you recommend to the congregation of your chosen context? Answer by doing the following:

   i. In a bulleted list, name the titles of five to ten books you recommend that are already published in the target language.

ii. Rank these titles by priority of reading for each type of reader above, marking the three ranking categories (new believers = 1N, 2N, 3N, etc.; believers from other churches = 1O, 2O, 3O, etc.; future church leaders = 1L, 2L, 3L, etc.) next to each title.

iii. List the titles of books you would like to see translated into the target language for use in the church plant. Consider this a short list you could someday suggest to potential translators and publishers in the country or language you plan to serve.

3. On a separate sheet of paper, create a table of Bible verses describing the benefits of God's Word to believers, along with the specific benefits that each mentions. Based on these passages, describe below your table what challenges believers would face if they didn't have access to Scripture in their native tongue.

Engaging the Outcast

Biblical Missions and Compassion

Textbook Content

CHAPTER 54: Compassion and Commission: Proclaiming the Gospel to "the Poor," by Mark Tatlock

> **INSERT 54.1:** Three Approaches to Compassion Ministries: Maintaining a Biblical Approach, by Brian Biedebach

> **INSERT 54.2:** Compassionate Evangelism: Toward Best Practices, by Shannon Hurley

CHAPTER 55: Thinking Biblically about Poverty and Spirituality, by Faly Ravoahangy

> **INSERT 55.1:** Helping without Hurting: Turning Challenges into Opportunities When Showing Mercy, by Lisa LaGeorge and Dave Phillips

Key Memory Verse

Listen, my beloved brothers: did not God choose the poor of this world to be rich in faith and heirs of the kingdom which He promised to those who love Him?

—JAMES 2:5

Additional Memory Verses

- Proverbs 14:31
- Mark 2:17
- Galatians 6:9–10
- Ephesians 5:1
- James 1:27

Scriptures for Further Meditation

- Matthew 5:13–16; Luke 19:10; Romans 5:8; James 2:14–17

Summary of Textbook Content

As recipients of God's undeserved mercy, Christians have the distinct opportunity to display God's compassion to those in need. The poor and helpless are providentially positioned to understand their need for the gospel, and this reality must not be overlooked by the local church. However, churches must also beware of compromising the Great Commission tasks of evangelism and discipleship with an unbalanced approach to mercy ministries. Remaining faithful requires a firm grounding in biblical principles of poverty and wealth, as well as great discernment concerning whom to minister to and how to help them in the best possible way.

Learning Objectives

- Acknowledge the connection between care for the poor and genuine faith in the gospel.
- Identify when social outreach loses proper biblical balance with evangelism.
- Obtain a biblical view of wealth and poverty.
- Recognize some of the common pitfalls when engaging in compassion ministries.

> Christ showed mercy to the poor while preaching to the poor, but His priority was gospel proclamation. That same priority should be emulated today—coupling the commission to evangelize with a compassion to help those who need it desperately.
>
> **—Mark Tatlock, "Compassion and Commission: Proclaiming the Gospel to 'the Poor'"**

Recall and Reflect

1. Summarize the three approaches to compassion ministries. [Biedebach, "Three Approaches to Compassion Ministries"]

2. What is the potential downside of the "**holistic**" approach to missions? [Biedebach, "Three Approaches to Compassion Ministries"]

3. What are the three best practices to remember when engaging in compassionate evangelism? [Hurley, "Compassionate Evangelism"]

4. What sins concerning money are a temptation for both the rich and the poor? What is the difference in how those sins are manifested? [Ravoahangy, "Thinking Biblically about Poverty and Spirituality"]

5. What is a **mercy ministry**, and what are its goals? [LaGeorge and Phillips, "Helping without Hurting"]

6. What arc the three different types of aid that mercy ministries often engage in, and what are the differences between them? [LaGeorge and Phillips, "Helping without Hurting"]

Analyze

1. Use Scripture to present the case that Christians ought to be characterized by extending compassion to those in need.

2. What is the local church's responsibility to extend compassion to those in need? How should the responsibilities of the individual Christian versus the local church be balanced?

3. What is the danger that occurs when compassion and commission are separated?

4. How are the poor in a better position than the rich to understand the gospel?

5. How does a lack of compassion for the poor hinder the believer's gospel witness?

6. What does it mean to say that mercy ministry is "the means" of evangelism and not "the mission"? What does this distinction look like when put into practice?

7. Considering that there are many opportunities around us to extend mercy, how should a church go about identifying which people to assist?

Implement

1. Consider the mercy that God extended to you when you had no ability to save yourself. How does His mercy toward you motivate you to extend mercy to others? Share your testimony with someone who is currently in the same condition you were before God saved you. Provide a summary of the encounter.

2. What is your mentality when you encounter a beggar on the street? Does your response reflect or contradict God's approach toward you?

3. What opportunities do you have in your current context to manifest compassion toward those in need?

4. What faulty views toward money are you most inclined toward (e.g., discontentment, stinginess, distrustfulness, jealousy, materialism)? What biblical truths do you need to meditate on in order to combat these sinful attitudes?

5. Evaluate your current giving practices in light of Scripture (e.g., 2 Cor 8–9). How do they measure up to biblical principles?

6. Have you encountered any situations where extending physical assistance was actually harmful rather than helpful? How do you make that determination? How do you respond to someone when you think physical assistance is not helping?

7. What are some initial steps you would take to identify the needs of the poor in your community?

Ask a Missionary

1. Are there any mercy ministries in your church? What is your approach toward those ministries, and how do you ensure biblical priorities in them?

2. What religious groups in your context are most involved in attempting to reach the poor in your society, and what appear to be their motivations? In your estimation, how do their practices and motives match the biblical approach to mercy ministry?

3. What unbiblical views toward money are most prevalent in your context? How have you attempted to shepherd people in these areas?

4. How do you identify which families to support with benevolence? How do you determine when material support should no longer be provided?

5. How do you respond when a mercy ministry recipient is taking advantage of the church?

Study the Scriptures

1. Study Matthew 25:31–46 and read a commentary written from a premillennial perspective. If you're unsure of one, ask your elder or teacher for direction. What does this passage teach about the role of compassion in the life of the believer? How might these future examples of compassion emphasized in this passage be manifested in believers' lives today?

> The end goal of mercy ministry in the local church is demonstrating the gospel message in word and deed to those being served.
>
> —Lisa LaGeorge and Dave Phillips, "Helping without Hurting: Turning Challenges into Opportunities When Showing Mercy"

2. Thoughtfully read both Romans 5:6–11 and Ephesians 2:1–10. How is the situation of the physically poor analogous to what is described of all individuals within these passages?

3. What truths are taught in Galatians 6:1–10 that compel the believer to lovingly sacrifice for his fellow brothers and sisters in the church?

4. Review the historical context of 2 Corinthians 8–9 by reading the notes of a study Bible or commentary. How do the churches of Macedonia contrast with the church at Corinth? How does this background contribute to your understanding of Paul's instruction in these chapters?

Missions Research

1. Compare the distinctives of three organizations that seem to conduct similar activities of compassion ministry in a country, region, or community of your choosing. Complete the table below. An organization's online mission statement is a good place to begin finding partial answers.

Distinctives	Organization #1:	Organization #2:	Organization #3:
Ministry activities			
Core convictions, principles, and theological commitments			
Definition or understanding of the gospel			
Approach to evangelism and discipleship			
Approach to and relationship with local churches			
Definition of mission success			

2. Trace the history of one of the missions organizations you evaluated in the prior research project. Describe the ministry's earliest practices, and compare those practices to their current activities. Indicate if, based on your research, there has been a shift in activities, emphases, doctrines, or philosophy of ministry in any direction.

3. Choose a historically revered missionary whose compassionate ministry helped to reduce or abolish an evil practice in society and bore fruit for proclamation ministry. Such information can be found in many missionary biographies and autobiographies. Summarize the missionary's motivations for mercy ministry, his or her core doctrinal convictions that shaped their social activities, those activities themselves, the response of the nationals, and how the mercy ministry aided evangelism and church planting, among other proclamation ministries, such as Bible translation and theological education.

Application Projects

1. Consider one potential mercy ministry that a local church in your area might implement for the poor of their community. Draft a philosophy of ministry document that connects doctrine and practice that could be used to support such a ministry. Include answers to the following questions:
   a. What are its objectives and aims?
   b. What are its priorities?
   c. How should the ministry be conducted?
   d. What might the program agenda look like, and how will the schedule reflect a balance between actions of mercy and of proclamation?
   e. Who should participate in the ministry, and how will they be evaluated and trained?
   f. How prominent should the ministry be in the life of the church?
   g. What Scripture passages would be used as the foundation for the ministry and the basis for its goals?
   h. What other questions should be considered?

2. Request a list from (or offer to compose a list for) your local church or from your missions sending organization containing the following information: number of supported missionaries, their locations (or regions, if the location is sensitive), their duration of service, their type or category of ministry, and a brief description of their ministries. Then determine the percentage breakdown of missionaries dedicated primarily to proclamation ministries and those dedicated primarily to supportive and/or compassion ministries, and collect this data into a one-page presentation. With the humble attitude of a learner, ask the leadership to help you understand if you have rightly captured the distribution of ministries they support and their rationale behind it.

> Saving and sanctifying grace causes believers to set their affections on things above.
> It motivates them to abound in generosity in response to God's abundant gifts.
>
> **—Faly Ravoahangy, "Thinking Biblically about Poverty and Spirituality"**

LESSON 20

Helping the Weak

Biblical Missions in Urban Ministry, Justice, Adoption, and Health Care

Textbook Content

CHAPTER 56: Reaching the Global City, by John Freiberg

CHAPTER 57: Portraits of Urban Ministry Past and Present, by John Freiberg

CHAPTER 58: Pursuing Justice: Representing God, the Defender of the Helpless in Cruel and Unjust Societies, by George A. Crawford

CHAPTER 59: At-Risk Children and How Adoption Displays the Gospel, by Mark Tatlock

    INSERT 59.1: A Street Kid Named Handsome, by David Beakley

CHAPTER 60: Health Care Missions as a Discipleship Strategy, by Carlan Wendler

    INSERT 60.1: Medical and Urban Ministry in a Muslim Majority City, by Ava Flores

    INSERT 60.2: Evangelism in a Burundi Hospital, by Carlan Wendler

Key Memory Verse

Yahweh is near to the brokenhearted
    and saves those who are crushed in
        spirit.

—PSALM 34:18

Additional Memory Verses

- Deuteronomy 10:17–18
- Psalm 68:5–6
- Matthew 9:35–36
- Titus 3:14
- James 4:17

Scriptures for Further Meditation

- Isaiah 5:16; Psalm 103:1–5; John 13:34–35;
  1 Corinthians 13:1; 1 John 3:18

Summary of Textbook Content

The gospel message itself is the only means by which one can be saved and thus the only real remedy to society's evils. Nevertheless, acts of benevolence do provide believers a much-needed platform to speak truth about Christ to those whom God has prepared to hear it. Whether countering the injustices of our world, providing a safe home to children at risk, or offering healing from physical ailments, Christians are called to show forth with their lives the gospel message they proclaim with their mouths. Social benevolence never replaces the proclamation of the gospel, but it does provide a clear demonstration of the gospel.

Learning Objectives

- Understand the strategic importance of cities for gospel advancement historically and in the present time.
- Identify obstacles to urban ministry and obtain biblical strategies to overcome them.
- Grasp the biblical definitions of justice and injustice.
- Obtain criteria for deciding when to confront injustice in a ministry context.
- Realize the modern societal trends that contribute to the need for adoption.
- Understand the biblical theology of adoption.
- Evaluate the unique opportunities and pitfalls of health care missions.
- Understand the relationship between sociopolitical responsibility and gospel proclamation.

> Good deeds without the good news
> are, ultimately, of no good use.
>
> **—George A. Crawford, "Pursuing Justice: Representing God, the Defender of the Helpless in Cruel and Unjust Societies"**

Recall and Reflect

1. What are the three types of cities discussed by Freiberg? [Freiberg, "Reaching the Global City"]

2. What opportunities should motivate a Christian to boldly proclaim the gospel in the city? [Freiberg, "Reaching the Global City"]

3. How did Irenaeus's life exemplify the practical implications of Christ's incarnation? [Freiberg, "Portraits of Urban Ministry Past and Present"]

4. What were the conditions under which Basil of Caesarea ministered? [Freiberg, "Portraits of Urban Ministry Past and Present"]

5. According to Crawford, what does injustice result from? [Crawford, "Pursuing Justice"]

6. According to Crawford, what must the missionary do beyond proclaiming God's concern for the oppressed? [Crawford, "Pursuing Justice"]

7. Which Old Testament account describes a servant beseeching a king for the release of an unlawfully detained prisoner? What lessons can be learned from this section of Scripture? [Crawford, "Pursuing Justice"]

8. What does it mean for a kid to be "at risk," and what are the different categories of "at-risk" kids? [Tatlock, "At-Risk Children and How Adoption Displays the Gospel"]

9. How might some efforts to improve orphanages unintentionally make the situation worse? What can orphanages do to mitigate this problem? [Tatlock, "At-Risk Children and How Adoption Displays the Gospel"]

10. What biblical precedents exist for combining health care with missions? [Wendler, "Health Care Missions as a Discipleship Strategy"]

11. Summarize the three pitfalls to avoid in health care missions. [Wendler, "Health Care Missions as a Discipleship Strategy"]

Analyze

1. How does having a robust **ecclesiology** impact ministry in urban settings?

2. What is the biblical basis for prioritizing cities in the effort to fulfill the Great Commission?

3. Freiberg provides four current examples of urban ministry. How do these examples demonstrate the unique opportunities urban ministry provides that are absent in more sprawled out areas?

4. How might social action or inaction have an impact on the credibility of a missionary's character?

5. When does the grammatical-historical interpretation of a passage provide an application directly to injustice?

6. Compare physical adoption with spiritual adoption. What components are similar? Which are unique?

7. Explain how adoptive parents can use their adoption as a tool for explaining the gospel to their children.

8. What does the doctrine of adoption communicate to believers that the doctrine of justification does not?

9. How does the doctrine of adoption relate to the doctrine of sanctification?

10. What unique opportunities for discipleship does health care provide?

> The Christian disciple-maker must think through which of his rights and privileges are actually obstacles to service, how to lay them aside and identify as much as possible with those he is called to serve, all without compromising fidelity to the truth.
>
> **—John Freiberg, "Portraits of Urban Ministry Past and Present"**

11. The Burundi hospital story provides an example of someone who cared for every aspect of a woman's situation (urgent physical suffering, separation from God as an unbeliever, and spiritual growth as a new believer). What would be the outcome of prioritizing one of these components at the expense of the others?

Implement

1. How can you better represent Christ when responding to those who are suffering?

2. What are some ways you can use your skills or talents as a platform for ministry?

3. How can the local church come alongside parents who have brought orphans into their homes?

4. How would you encourage an adoptive parent struggling with some of the challenges of adoption?

Ask a Missionary

1. What opportunities have you had to care for the sick or dying? How have you grown in this capacity? What advice would you share with those who have little experience ministering in this way?

2. What injustices have you observed on your mission field?

3. What criteria do you use when considering how to act against injustice?

4. What are some ways you have seen human suffering lead to opportunities for the gospel?

5. Are there any families in your congregation with adopted children? What challenges have they faced? How has the local church been able to help?

6. Does your local church engage in outreach ministry to urban cities? If so, what fruit have you observed from this ministry? What are some of the specific challenges you have encountered?

Study the Scriptures

1. Study Proverbs 18:13 and 19:2. How do these passages assist a missionary in evaluating a problem before taking action? What other proverbs or commands from Scripture would you add?

> We are called to love one another no less than how Christ has loved us. Not only is the ground level at the foot of the cross, but all heads are level at the foot of the cross.
>
> **—David Beakley, "A Street Kid Named Handsome"**

2. How might 2 Corinthians 5:10 motivate a missionary to fight injustice?

3. How was the crisis concerning Greek-speaking Jewish widows resolved in Acts 6:1–7? What example does this set for missionaries today?

4. Study the passages that address the doctrine of adoption, such as Romans 8:12–17; Galatians 4:1–7; and Ephesians 1:3–6. Use a concordance or Bible software to find other Scriptures that teach on God's fatherhood and the believer's sonship to Him. How is your understanding of your relationship to God shaped by these passages?

5. Evaluate the relationship between Jesus' words and His works in the Gospels (e.g., Matt 4:23; 9:35). Summarize the relationship. Did one take priority over the other? What was the role of each?

Missions Research

1. Research one specific urban ministry that is known for being a biblically faithful initiative of members of the community or of nearby local churches. If possible, interview people who have participated in that ministry, and respond to these prompts:
   a. What are some of the challenges that the ministry faces reaching its target population?

   b. How have they used those difficulties as opportunities for the gospel?

   c. What fruit have they seen from striving to do ministry faithfully?

   d. If your local church elders do not already have a philosophy of urban ministry documented, ask for an opportunity to present your findings to them to assist with prayer and possibly finding new avenues for ministry.

2. Look further into the life of William Carey and discover how he combated biblical injustice while upholding the biblical priority of gospel proclamation. Explore his other innovative projects for the people to whom he proclaimed Christ beyond that of abolishing *sati*. Then research and describe one other missionary activity in India today that complements proclamation ministry in a way that William Carey might approve. Summarize your findings.

3. Every day, people are bought, sold, and abused. Research human trafficking in a country, such as Nepal or Turkmenistan, or a region, such as Central Asia or North Africa. Do the following tasks:
   a. Provide details of the main forms of exploitation and the types of people enslaved to report on the scope of the problem of human trafficking.

   b. Document a variety of ways that missionaries have taken public action on the forms of trafficking in that country or region.

   c. Draw from some of the stories missionaries and evangelical ministries have shared in that country, region, or other locations to identify what seem to be some best practices for evangelizing and discipling the trafficked people they have rescued.

Application Projects

1. Use the following table to create a list of categories of at-risk children (e.g., orphaned kids, street kids, kids with disabilities, kids in war zones). How can the biblical principles of hospitality apply specifically to each category?

At-Risk Category	Principle	Application

2. In a separate document write out a philosophy of ministry to those with physical and developmental disabilities that could be used for your local church. Include a list of training resources, books, and support organizations that exist in your country or might be allowed into your country. If your church already has a disabilities ministry, interview the ministry leader about the blessings and challenges of the ministry, and offer to help develop the resource list and possibly become more involved in the ministry.

3. Proclamation and demonstration go hand in hand. How would you balance meeting practical needs as you proclaim the gospel in your community? Fill in the following table by listing in the first column tangible problems or needs that the poor or oppressed in your society experience; in the second column, potential activities that might lead to gospel proclamation; and in the third column, a key concept from the gospel message or about the character of Jesus appropriate to the problem or need to accompany the activity.

Problem or Need	Potential Activity	Gospel Concept
Hunger	Regular free lunch event at local church with music, evangelistic sermon.	Jesus is "the bread of life" to all who come to Him by faith (John 6:35).

Reaching the World

Biblical Missions through Education, Hospitality, and Vocation

Textbook Content

CHAPTER 61: Global Opportunities through Education: Advantages, Trends, and Issues, by Mark D. Rentz

> **INSERT 61.1:** Seeking the Educational Well-Being of the City, by Peter Olivetan
>
> **INSERT 61.2:** From Book Tables to Church Pews: Effective Campus Ministry in Lilongwe, Malawi, by Chisomo Masambuka

CHAPTER 62: Imitating God's Gracious Invitation: Biblical Hospitality and the Gospel, by Mark Tatlock

> **INSERT 62.1:** The Missionary Wife and Hospitality, by Shelbi Cullen
>
> **INSERT 62.2:** The World in Our Backyard: Local Outreach to International Student Communities, by Mark D. Rentz
>
> **INSERT 62.3:** Evangelism to Indian Medical Students in the Philippines, by Devraj Urs

CHAPTER 63: The Marketplace Believer: Ambassadors for Christ on the Clock, by Eric Weathers

> **INSERT 63.1:** Building a Corporation in Ethiopia to Reach the Nations, by Abera Ajula
>
> **INSERT 63.2:** The Call to Local Cross-Cultural Outreach, by Mark Tatlock

Key Memory Verse

Be hospitable to one another without grumbling. As each one has received a gift, employ it in serving one another as good stewards of the manifold grace of God—whoever speaks, as one speaking the oracles of God; whoever serves, as one serving by the strength which God supplies; so that in all things God may be glorified through Jesus Christ, to whom belongs the glory and might forever and ever. Amen.

—1 PETER 4:9–11

Additional Memory Verses

- Jeremiah 29:7
- 1 Corinthians 9:19–22
- Ephesians 6:5–9
- Colossians 3:23–24
- 1 Timothy 2:1–4

Scriptures for Further Meditation

- Matthew 22:37–39; John 4:35; Romans 12:17–21; Hebrews 13:2; Ephesians 5:18–21

Summary of Textbook Content

The interconnected world in which we live today is a drastically different landscape than was seen in past generations. In the midst of this increasingly diverse environment are unique opportunities to fulfill the Great Commission wherever we are. Whether educators, businesspeople, church leaders, or simply hospitable believers, Christians today can integrate their evangelistic witness into their vocations and local communities in order to proclaim the excellencies of Christ to the global harvest that God has brought straight to their doorstep. Ultimately, we all are called to live as ambassadors for Christ in our sphere of influence, imitating God's gracious invitation through the creative use of our gifts and opportunities to make disciples of all nations.

Learning Objectives

- Recognize globalization as a unique opportunity to make disciples of unreached people groups.
- Recognize the global demand for education and the gospel opportunity it provides.
- Understand which current trends in education afford opportunities for missions.
- Recognize the importance of the local church when doing campus outreach.
- Understand biblical **hospitality** and its practical implementation.
- Identify key character qualities that ensure effective gospel witness in the workplace.

> Scripture indicates that hospitality is usually demonstrating kindness toward strangers who are unable to reciprocate. It exemplifies God's own character and His greatest demonstration of unmerited kindness: the love of Christ in coming, living, dying, and rising again to pardon sinners (spiritual strangers) who had no ability to repay Him. Hospitality should illustrate the gospel's one-sidedness.
>
> —Mark Tatlock, "Imitating God's Gracious Invitation: Biblical Hospitality and the Gospel"

Recall and Reflect

1. What are the current global trends that provide opportunities for missions-minded educators? [Rentz, "Global Opportunities through Education"]

2. What are the challenges of which Christian educators serving overseas need to be aware? [Rentz, "Global Opportunities through Education"]

3. Summarize the six advantages Paul had that enabled him to effectively plant churches in so many different geographical regions. [Rentz, "Global Opportunities through Education"]

4. What are four ways Christians can engage in disciple-making by pursuing the educational well-being of others? [Olivetan, "Seeking the Educational Well-Being of the City"]

5. What issues arise as a result of college campus ministry not being tied to the local church? [Masambuka, "From Book Tables to Church Pews"]

6. What is the meaning of the Greek word for "hospitality" (*philoxenia*)? [Tatlock, "Imitating God's Gracious Invitation"]

7. How was personal hospitality practiced in the ancient world, and why has the perceived need for it diminished in the world today? [Tatlock, "Imitating God's Gracious Invitation"]

8. Provide a simple, one-sentence definition of biblical hospitality. [Tatlock, "Imitating God's Gracious Invitation"]

9. What unique means has God provided for allowing people from the 10/40 window to be evangelized elsewhere? [Rentz, "The World in Our Backyard"]

10. What components of work do the Christian employee and the Christian employer share in common? [Weathers, "The Marketplace Believer"]

11. What does the phrase "serving with good will" (Eph 6:7) mean, and what is the biblical motivation for this directive? [Weathers, "The Marketplace Believer"]

12. Which characteristic of being Spirit-filled in Ephesians 5:18–21 is particularly important for being a marketplace minister, and why? [Weathers, "The Marketplace Believer"]

Analyze

1. In what ways do the current trends in education provide opportunities for Christians to reach more difficult regions of the world than have historically been available?

2. How might a missionary be tempted to lose focus on his primary mission? What measures should be in place to help prevent this?

3. How does God's command for Judah to seek the peace of Babylon (Jer 29:7) instruct the way Christians should live within pagan societies?

4. Why are foreign students particularly ideal recipients for biblical hospitality?

> The greatest profit, beyond participating in the gospel's expansion through one's business efforts, is something that is only realized at the end of this age.
>
> —Abera Ajula, "Building a Corporation in Ethiopia to Reach the Nations"

5. What is the biblical way to think about "friendship evangelism"?

6. How might "having fellow believers over for a meal" not necessarily be an expression of biblical hospitality?

7. Why do most people think that hospitality is the domain of women? Why and how should this perspective be changed?

8. How does one's understanding of himself as an "alien and stranger" motivate him to practice hospitality?

Implement

1. How can your local church engage in outreach on a college campus?

2. What educational opportunities can you think of (occupations, ministries, events, etc.) in your current context that would provide a clear platform either to present the gospel directly or make individual disciples?

3. How can Christians who are not in vocational ministry serve and support university ministries?

4. What can you do to be a more God-honoring worker in your current context? Think of every aspect of what you do on the job.

5. How might your handling of your finances and/or possessions change if you fully embrace the reality that everything you own really belongs to the Lord?

6. What are some creative ways business owners can steward company profits toward the Great Commission?

7. What are some ways you can be more hospitable in your own life? To whom would you like to extend hospitality? What specific acts of kindness can you offer?

8. Are there any foreign populations in the area where you live? What are some practical steps you can take personally to reach out to those people?

9. What steps can your church take to be more accommodating to foreigners who don't speak English as their first language?

Ask a Missionary

1. Have recent trends in education affected your missionary endeavors positively or negatively? What opportunities or challenges are presented by such trends?

2. Are there any educational opportunities in the country you serve that might open the door to extend the gospel directly or indirectly?

3. Does your ministry engage in any outreach to university students? What worldview clashes do you most typically encounter when interacting with them? What practical steps have helped you to reach university students with the truth?

4. What do you and, if applicable, your family do to practice hospitality to those around you? In what ways did you have to adapt to the surrounding culture in order to be more effective at hospitality?

5. Explain how you shepherd those in your congregation and local ministry network to understand how to serve Christ in their vocations.

6. How do you personally strive to model a good work ethic toward those you serve?

Study the Scriptures

1. Study Jeremiah 29:1–14. What did it mean for the exiles to "seek the peace of the city," and why was this important? Search the book of Daniel to identify how the exiles attempted to obey this command.

2. Study Ephesians 6:5–9. What principles can you draw from this passage about how we are to approach our jobs? Why would these principles be important to serve God successfully on the mission field?

3. Study the story of the good Samaritan in Luke 10:25–37. What principles of hospitality do you derive from this text?

4. Study James 2:1–13. How was the attitude of the believers described in this passage contrary to biblical teaching on hospitality?

5. Study the lives of Priscilla and Aquila as recorded in Acts 18; Romans 16:3; 1 Corinthians 16:19; and 2 Timothy 4:19. Record their locations and timeline information from the biblical data. For help consult a Bible dictionary containing an entry for this couple. Describe the effect that their displacement from their home had on their vocation, their ministry with Paul, Apollos, Timothy, and the believers in Asia Minor. What inspires you about their attitude and involvement in ministry, given their life circumstances?

Missions Research

1. Identify some biblically aligned churches that have well-organized international outreach ministries in their immediate areas. Investigate what they do to reach those communities. If possible, speak with one of their leaders to gain practical advice on how to successfully evangelize and disciple foreign populations locally. Summarize your findings below.

2. Research how hospitality is practiced in a specific cultural setting of interest to you, both among believers and unbelievers. In what ways are their practices of hospitality congruent or incongruent with the biblical model of hospitality? How do your findings differ between believers and unbelievers?

3. In a separate document create a resource list of biblical worldview training programs, books, or online seminars that you could share with university students you might disciple. The goal of the resources is to help students discern the moral, ethical, spiritual, and antibiblical themes so often presented in university classrooms. List the resources by topic and theme.

4. Read the mission statements of multiple Christian universities, Bible colleges, and Bible institutes in your country or chosen field of service. Then do the following:
   a. For each institution type, rank the schools by what you perceive to be their degree of biblical fidelity, with the most biblically faithful being first in each list.

b. Explain your ranking method and criteria.

c. Read information on the program and/or courses offered at these schools on global missions (e.g., global or intercultural studies, evangelism, outreach, the role of the local church). Do the missions emphases seem to match the educational goals and purposes of the institution? Identify any emphases that might have veered from the priority of biblical missions.

Application Projects

1. Identify local educational institutions and determine who and how they support international students. Develop a proposal for how your local church could actively reach international students at these institutions, and articulate it in a one-page presentation.

2. Do a performance review of yourself in your current occupation. Conduct this review as if Jesus were your immediate supervisor and your evaluation included biblical principles such as those laid out in Ephesians 6:5–9. Answer the following questions based on these criteria, and share your answers with an elder, discipler, or trusted Christian friend:
a. What are my accomplishments for Christ's kingdom?

b. What areas need improvement?

c. What steps can I take to improve these areas?

d. What final rating would you give yourself as a Christian employee serving under the Lord Christ?

> A growing worldwide demand for education and specialized skill training
> has created a wave of opportunities for Christian educators to integrate
> their work and witness for the purpose of world evangelism.
>
> **—Mark D. Rentz, "Global Opportunities through Education: Advantages, Trends, and Issues"**

3. Perform a job hunt and find ten missions opportunities or job postings, either short term or long term, where your vocational expertise could be employed to support missions. Start by reading the websites or print materials of several missions agencies with which you are like-minded. List the opportunities and organizations, rank them, and state your reasons for each ranking. Do not limit yourself to a preferred country or cultural context.

4. Join a university-student evangelism and discipleship ministry that is under your local church or take the first steps to propose one. (Even if you do not have a university nearby, students return home for school breaks, and believers need contact with their home churches while away at school.) Fill in the following table to identify the unique needs and challenges that exist when reaching out to university-aged students, as well as possible ways to meet the needs and overcome the challenges.

Ministry	Student Needs	Challenges	Plan to Meet Needs/ Overcome Challenges
Evangelism			
Discipleship			

LESSON 22

Best Practices for Effective Short-Term Ministries

Textbook Content

CHAPTER 64: Short-Term Ministries, Not Short-Term Missions, by Rodney Andersen

> **INSERT 64.1:** Anatomy of a Short-Term Ministry Trip: Purpose, Impact, Planning, and Training, by David E. Bosworth

CHAPTER 65: Examining Short-Term Missions in Modern Church History, by Lisa LaGeorge

CHAPTER 66: Difficult-to-Access Ministry Trips: Principles from the Alaskan Bush, by Nathan Schneider, with Jeff Crotts and Randy Karlberg

Key Memory Verse

For even the Son of Man did not come to be served, but to serve, and to give His life a ransom for many.

—MARK 10:45

Additional Memory Verses

- Romans 12:9–13
- 1 Corinthians 15:58
- 2 Corinthians 9:12
- Hebrews 6:10
- 1 Peter 4:10

Scripture for Further Meditation

- Acts 11:19–24; Philippians 2:25–30; Colossians 3:23–24

Summary of Textbook Content

Short-term ministries (STMs) have the potential to play a much-needed role in supporting missionaries and strengthening churches abroad. While biblical precedents exist, the practice of short-term ministries has exploded in recent years, requiring a fresh, critical look at this increasingly popular trend. Though the potential benefits for everyone involved can be immense, the harm STMs can bring is just as real. Thus, STMs should not be approached casually by adventurous youth merely seeking to boost their spiritual growth or interest in missions. Rather, they should be carefully planned by sending churches in coordination with the missionary overseas, and STM participants should be thoughtfully selected and diligently prepared by church leaders to ensure optimal success. All short-term ministries should be conducted with long-term goals in mind in order to bear lasting fruit.

Learning Objectives

- Distinguish "short-term ministries" from "short-term missions" in concept and practice.
- Recognize how to measure the success of an STM.
- Identify how STMs are tied to the Great Commission.
- Appreciate the benefits that STMs can have for missionaries and their ministries as well as participants and their sending churches.
- Understand the harm that STMs can cause missionaries and their ministries overseas.
- Obtain strategies to maximize the benefit and minimize the harm of an STM through careful planning and preparation.

> Although short-term ministries are not a replacement for the work of missionaries, they can complement the work that is being done by those missionaries. This starts with seeing the ministry and the ongoing work of the missionary as the main beneficiary of these STM teams rather than the participants.
>
> **—Rodney Andersen, "Short-Term Ministries, Not Short-Term Missions"**

Recall and Reflect

1. Why is "ministries" a better label than "missions" for sending out a team of church members on short-term assignments? [Andersen, "Short-Term Ministries, Not Short-Term Missions"]

2. Who should be the target beneficiary of the STM trip, and why? [Andersen, "Short-Term Ministries, Not Short-Term Missions"]

4. Summarize some of the potential drawbacks to short-term ministries. [Andersen, "Short-Term Ministries, Not Short-Term Missions"; LaGeorge, "Examining Short-Term Missions in Modern Church History"]

5. What three groups should be debriefed for evaluating the effectiveness of an STM soon afterward? [Andersen, "Short-Term Ministries, Not Short-Term Missions"]

6. What is a "specific vision" when it comes to STMs? How will it help the leader of an STM in the preparation process? [Bosworth, "Anatomy of a Short-Term Ministry Trip"]

7. How might screening potential STM team members affect the success of the trip? [Bosworth, "Anatomy of a Short-Term Ministry Trip"]

8. Who is potentially affected by STMs? [LaGeorge, "Examining Short-Term Missions in Modern Church History"]

9. What components of STMs to remote Alaskan villages has the Lord used to open villagers up to the gospel? [Schneider, Crotts, and Karlberg, "Difficult-to-Access Ministry Trips"]

10. What is the long-term goal for the rural Alaskan communities, for which STM teams have helped to lay the groundwork? [Schneider, Crotts, and Karlberg, "Difficult-to-Access Ministry Trips"]

Analyze

1. Why are STMs not a substitute for missions or missionaries?

2. What are direct and indirect ways that STMs link to the Great Commission?

3. What biblical criteria should be used for screening potential STM participants?

4. What could an STM leader do to help minimize the potential dangers of a trip?

5. Why should the STM leader be a man of proven character and leadership? What tasks must he perform that require a high level of spiritual maturity?

6. Why should churches not send young or struggling believers who need a jump start to their spiritual walk on STMs?

7. Why should the receiving missionary be the one to determine what activities the STM will perform?

8. Why is reporting back to the sending church important after an STM is completed?

9. Why must STM strategies appreciate that there is no "one-size-fits-all" approach to missions? How could a false assumption here impede a ministry's effectiveness, for example, in various villages of the Alaskan bush?

Implement

1. Considering the potential for STMs to bring great benefit or cause great harm, what are some types of trips that could bring benefit to the missionary and his or her ministry?

2. If you were an STM leader, how would you plan for and implement the discipleship of team members on the trip? Be specific.

3. What do you think should be addressed during an STM debrief? What questions would you ask participants if you were leading one?

4. Have you ever been on an STM? What were the challenges on the trip? What impact did the trip have on the long-term ministry in the target location? What impact did it have on you personally?

5. What spiritual challenges should you guard against on an STM? What could you do to avoid those pitfalls, and how would you respond if and when they surface?

Ask a Missionary

1. Do you view STMs as helpful, hurtful, or something in between?

2. Did you participate in any STMs before becoming a missionary? If so, did they contribute to your decision to become one?

3. How have STMs benefited your missionary work abroad? In what ways have they assisted you in your personal or family needs?

4. What would you want sending churches to know about engaging in STMs?

5. How have you assessed the physical dangers or threats when preparing for ministry trips in a given region?

Study the Scriptures

1. Examine Acts 9:23–25 and 2 Corinthians 11:23–27. How do these passages demonstrate Paul's willingness to move into dangerous situations but also his care to avoid risk of harm to himself? How can the missionary today model this same pattern?

2. How can James 4:13–15 shape the attitude of a missionary toward planning projects and strategizing ministry? How about the attitude of an STM leader?

3. Review 2 Corinthians 8:18–21. Make a list of practical applications from this model of how to exercise "transparent integrity" in collecting funds for missions.

4. According to Ephesians 4:11–16, what are the means that Christ uses to mature His church? What is the ultimate result, according to verse 13? In light of this, how does a short-term ministry build the body of Christ in love (v. 16)?

Missions Research

1. Conduct research on at least three of the agencies that focus on STMs, such as Youth With A Mission (YWAM), Operation Mobilization (OM), or Experience Mission (EM). Answer the following questions for each agency you research:
   a. In what ways does their vision and purpose align with biblical principles and priorities? In what ways might it not?

b. Who do the primary beneficiaries of their STM opportunities seem to be? Who are the secondary beneficiaries? Evaluate whether these emphases appear to align with the biblical practice of STMs, and how so.

c. Describe the pre-field training provided by each organization, particularly their training on the content and delivery of the gospel message, the use of Scripture in their activities, and the foundational theology they teach.

2. Choose three of the following categories of short-term ministries to investigate: construction, health care, orphan care, student and campus evangelism, pastoral training and theological instruction, administration help, and camp and conference service. Then do the following tasks:

a. Read a few reports or watch videos from a variety of participants in each of your chosen categories. Consider searching church and agency websites, social media, blogs, and newsletters. List each report you read or viewed and any pertinent reference information, so that it could be found again later.

b. List specific activities common to the participants of each of the ministries (e.g., establishing a pop-up health clinic in a village; distributing tracts on a college campus).

c. Summarize how the specific ministry activities of the STMs either led to or might not have led to opportunities to proclaim the gospel. (Keep in mind that not all reports and recordings demonstrate such direct connections, and your documentation here is not an evaluation of biblical faithfulness.)

d. Summarize the gospel proclamation activities themselves, gleaned either through their written statements or video and photo reports that portray evangelistic moments.

e. Detail the relationship the STM participants seemed to have with churches in the locations of their activities. State whether they appeared to interact with and involve local church leaders or members before, during, or after their activities.

Application Projects

This lesson has one major application project, divided into sequential steps that will assist you to potentially propose a short-term ministry trip to your local church.

1. Choose a ministry location from among the missionaries your local church supports (or is considering supporting).

   Answer the following questions:

   a. What is this ministry, and who are the missionaries?

   b. Why would this ministry benefit from receiving an STM team?

   c. Has this ministry received STM teams previously from your church or any supporting church? If so, attempt to state when and what the team(s) did. (Some information might have been reported in past missionary newsletters and church-wide communications.)

2. Interview the missionaries to learn what their experiences have been with STMs, whether individuals or teams for various lengths of time.

Ask them the following questions:

a. What made for the most effective short-term ministries?

b. Were there any projects or activities you would like to see repeated?

c. What made for the least effective short-term ministries?

d. What are some aspects or experiences you would like sending churches to make sure are never repeated?

e. What recommendations would you make so that future teams are more effective?

f. Would you grant permission for an STM team to be designed with your feedback and sent to you, even if only hypothetically? (If not, the student should consult their elder or missions leadership team for another candidate.)

3. Create a presentation that can be shared with the missionary, your church leadership, or possible STM participants, stating the basic information you collected and the information needed for your designed STM. Use the following to begin drafting the presentation's content.

Include the following information:

a. The main activity or activities you propose (e.g., construction, health care, evangelistic youth camp).

b. How you anticipate the trip will benefit the missionaries and their ministries.

c. What feedback and approval you have received from the missionaries in the planning process.

d. The ideal trip duration and top scheduling options (coordinate up to three options between the missionaries, your elders, and your missions leadership team).

e. Team information.
   i.   The number of teammates needed.

   ii. Biblical qualifications for believers in your local church to participate as teammates. Determine with your elders and missions leadership team if the participants must be formal members of the church, though at least it should be required that they be baptized according to the stipulations of believer's baptism.

   iii. The name of a man biblically qualified in character and skillset whom you suggest as the team leader.

4. If you have been approved by your church leaders to lead an actual short-term ministry trip, it is now time to invite the potential teammates and communicate all information gathered thus far.

   What to do:

   a. Seek their acceptance to join the team after praying, receiving counsel, and coordinating the trip scheduling options.
   b. Ensure that all potential teammates have read and understood the list of criteria for participating in an STM trip sponsored by your local church. (See "Criteria for Sponsoring a Short-Term Ministry Trip" at the end of this lesson.)

5. Meet with an elder or missions leadership team member to design the pre-trip training for your team.

Include the following:

a. Consider having teammates read the STM content of the *Biblical Missions* textbook and answer select questions from this workbook lesson. Consider other reading materials as well, either from the textbook or resources recommended by the church leadership, along with questions from other workbook lessons. Then schedule to have the team meet to discuss under the guidance of the team leader.

b. Set the number and tentative schedule of team meetings for fellowship, trip information, and prayer. Attempt videoconferencing with the missionaries in at least one meeting, if possible.

c. Compose a master pre-trip calendar incorporating your reading assignments, discussions, fellowships, and prayer meetings.

6. Sketch ideas for team meetings during and after the STM trip.

Attempt to answer the following, and ask your elders and missions leadership team members for feedback:

a. What kinds and what frequency of on-field meetings (e.g., missionary-led, informal, group, individual check-ins, inviting locals to participate, team-only) might facilitate the spiritual and emotional shepherding of the teammates as well as the successful continuance of the activities?

b. What are some of the components of these on-field meetings that you anticipate might be necessary regularly or occasionally (e.g., prayer, debriefing, instruction, sharing observations and experiences, Bible study, rebuke and counsel)? Provide some initial ideas of how these meetings might be conducted.

c. What kind of post-trip debriefing meeting(s) might be useful for the STM teammates, for the missionaries, and for the local church elders and missions leadership?

> Trust exists on a continuum, built slowly, broken quickly—particularly in cross-cultural missions.
>
> **—Nathan Schneider, with Jeff Crotts and Randy Karlberg,**
> **"Difficult-to-Access Ministry Trips: Principles from the Alaskan Bush"**

CRITERIA FOR SPONSORING A SHORT-TERM MINISTRY TRIP

To qualify as a church-sponsored, biblical, short-term ministry trip, the following criteria should be met:

- The trip must be approved by the missions leadership team.
- The trip must be led by a team leader approved by the missions leadership team.
- The trip must have a clearly defined scope of ministry that is connected to and desired by the ongoing ministry of a church-supported missionary or partner ministry.
- The trip must include sufficient preparation and training to effectively accomplish the ministry purpose.
- The team size and giftedness needed to effectively accomplish the ministry purpose must be determined by the missions leadership team.
- All team members must complete a short-term missions application process that ensures their spiritual qualifications.
- The individual team members must be approved by the team leader, missions leadership team, and/or the elders.

LESSON 23

Best Practices for Effective Ministry Partnerships

Textbook Content

CHAPTER 67: Can We Work Together? A Biblical Theology of Collaboration, by James Harmeling

> **INSERT 67.1:** The Partnership Strategies of Paul, Apostle to the Outskirts, by Chris Burnett

CHAPTER 68: Cooperation and Separation: Partnership in the Gospel Strategically and Selectively, by Tim Cantrell

> **INSERT 68.1:** The Conflicting Mission of the Church and Parachurch in India, by Sammy Williams

> **INSERT 68.2:** The Strategic Role of On-Air Preaching in Hostile Contexts, by Edward W. Cannon

> **INSERT 68.3:** Can You Find Me in the Forest? A Testimony of Media's Reach for the Gospel, by Nathan Giesbrecht

CHAPTER 69: Partnership Strategies in Africa with Local Leaders and Rural Communities, by Thomas Hodzi

Key Memory Verse

Therefore I, the prisoner in the Lord, exhort you to walk worthy of the calling with which you have been called, with all humility and gentleness, with patience, bearing with one another in love, being diligent to keep the unity of the Spirit in the bond of peace.

—EPHESIANS 4:1–3

Additional Memory Verses

- John 17:20–23
- Romans 14:19
- Ephesians 4:4–6
- 1 Timothy 6:20–21
- Hebrews 10:24–25

Scriptures for Further Meditation

- Acts 2:41–47; Romans 16:17–20; Colossians 3:12–15; 2 Timothy 1:12–14

Summary of Textbook Content

Christ's mandate in the Great Commission is too monumental for any one individual to accomplish. Thus, partnerships are not just important, they are necessary for any progress to be made. Yet, although collaboration is essential, it is not easy. God often draws unexpected people into His body in unexpected ways. Despite this diversity that God has wrought, when the gospel is central in belief and practice, unlikely partnerships are possible. At the same time, unity around the gospel requires a corresponding separation from the world. Great wisdom is required to know how to maintain integrity while advancing the light of the gospel in the dark world that surrounds us.

Learning Objectives

- Appreciate the diversity of individuals that God calls into the church.
- Recognize the importance of church unity.
- Understand the biblical basis for collaboration in the Great Commission.
- Grasp the centrality of the gospel in ministry partnerships.
- Identify the character necessary to maintain enduring partnerships.
- Discern the levels of doctrinal unity necessary in various contexts.
- Grasp the importance of local leaders in reaching difficult places with the gospel.

> Ministry teams will be only as effective as the convictions they share and upon which they act.
>
> **—James Harmeling, "Can We Work Together? A Biblical Theology of Collaboration"**

Recall and Reflect

1. What are five considerations to help maintain spiritual unity in collaboration? [Harmeling, "Can We Work Together?"]

2. What is the name of the church in Scripture that failed at collaboration? What was the cause of this failure? [Harmeling, "Can We Work Together?"]

3. What formed the basis of Paul's partnerships in his missionary endeavors? [Burnett, "The Partnership Strategies of Paul, Apostle to the Outskirts"]

4. What was the purpose of Paul's greetings in chapter 16 of the book of Romans? [Burnett, "The Partnership Strategies of Paul, Apostle to the Outskirts"]

5. What does Cantrell mean when he says that "separation from the world is a prerequisite for genuine unity in the body of Christ"? [Cantrell, "Cooperation and Separation"]

6. Who has the primary job of training pastors for ministry—seminaries or local churches? Defend your answer. [Cantrell, "Cooperation and Separation"]

7. What is the meaning of the word parachurch? [Williams, "The Conflicting Mission of the Church and Parachurch in India"]

8. What are the advantages of radio for places that are more difficult to reach with the gospel? [Cannon, "The Strategic Role of On-Air Preaching in Hostile Contexts"]

9. What are the three pillars that are essential to establishing an effective preaching ministry in difficult settings? [Cannon, "The Strategic Role of On-Air Preaching in Hostile Contexts"]

10. A missionary should be willing to say no to potential ministry opportunities that arise. What questions should be asked when considering, for example, whether to add a new mercy component to the church's ministry? [Hodzi, "Partnership Strategies in Africa with Local Leaders and Rural Communities"]

11. What are three common expectations or assumptions that African village leaders may have when missionaries enter their communities? [Hodzi, "Partnership Strategies in Africa with Local Leaders and Rural Communities"]

Analyze

1. Explain how the gospel is key to producing unifying love and fellowship among believers.

2. How should one balance a commitment to sound doctrine with the universality of spiritual fellowship expressed in Romans 16:16?

3. How might collaboration be affected by agreement on the central mission (gospel proclamation) yet disagreement on its execution?

4. In what ways can a "strong personality" be both a benefit and a liability for missionaries?

5. Explain how personal purity in one's private life leads to greater unity within the local church.

6. Explain the correct relationship between parachurch ministries and the local church. What are the limits, if any, of parachurch ministries? To what extent are they dependent on the local church?

7. The role of the missionary as elder requires the highest level of spiritual unity. Why is unity so important for a body of elders in a local church?

8. Why is it so important for radio preachers reaching closed-access areas to be indigenous speakers who possess local awareness? In what ways might the proclamation be hindered if these factors are not present?

9. How does Hodzi's chapter demonstrate the importance of being intimately acquainted with a particular culture in order to effectively reach it with the gospel? Why would an indigenous leader have a unique advantage in this effort?

> Spiritual fellowship in the body of Christ is visible, beginning with intentional relationships and leading to productive partnerships for the gospel out in the world.
>
> **—Chris Burnett, "The Partnership Strategies of Paul, Apostle to the Outskirts"**

10. Analyze the following purpose statement of one particular missions organization: "Through development, relief, and advocacy, we pursue fullness of life for every child by serving the poor and oppressed regardless of religion, race, ethnicity, or gender, as a demonstration of God's unconditional love for all people." What words or phrases might lead some missionaries to deprioritize proclamation ministries?

Implement

1. Think of someone you do ministry with. Based on the five considerations for maintaining spiritual unity discussed by Harmeling, what are some steps you can take to cultivate greater unity with that ministry partner?

2. Identify areas of your life in which you can grow in purity (thoughts, motives, speech, doctrine, etc.). In what ways might those areas be hindering your effectiveness in ministry?

3. Why should missionaries consider reaching those outside their target demographic or people group? What are some ways they can do this? What are some ways you can be sensitive to people around you that you would not normally target for ministry?

4. How might you practically prioritize your partner relationship in ministry?

5. How can you better "pursue the things which make for peace and the building up of one another" (Rom. 14:19)?

6. Imagine there is a church member who serves in a parachurch ministry. If he or she requested to make that ministry a formal partner with your church, what requirements would be set to forge such a partnership?

7. What would you say to someone who was involved in a parachurch ministry to orphans overseas and was not attending a local church?

8. Hodzi's essay demonstrates strategic planning in an effort to reach a particular community for the gospel. As you consider the people around you, what are some ways you can be more strategic in your own gospel efforts?

Ask a Missionary

1. Have you experienced any ministry partnership that didn't go well? If so, what was the source of the problem (as far as you can share)? Based on this experience, what advice would you offer to potential missionaries regarding the selection of ministry partners?

2. Have you been able to partner with other churches in your region that have a clear understanding of the gospel? Describe what these partnerships have looked like.

3. What advice would you give to the Western missionaries who have a task-oriented approach to missions? What about those who work with Western missionaries?

4. What practices have you established to help maintain unity among the elders in your church?

Study the Scriptures

1. Read 1 Corinthians 3:1–7. How did spiritual immaturity create division in the Corinthian church? Where else is the analogy of spiritual infancy used, and how?

2. Study the principles of body life discussed in Colossians 3:12–17. How can you cultivate these attitudes toward your current ministry partners? If these are not present in your life today, they are not likely to be present when you go to the mission field.

3. Do an extensive study of the principles of Christian relationships outlined in Romans 12:9–21. Use an expository or applicational commentary or two to grasp the poignance of each command in this passage. Consider which of these principles you need to apply in your existing relationships to produce greater unity with fellow believers, and summarize them below.

4. According to Ephesians 4:3, what does it mean to be "diligent to keep the unity of the Spirit in the bond of peace"?

5. Read Numbers 13:1–14:10. How does this section of Scripture highlight a "division of conviction"? Which parties were in the right? How do you know?

> Collaboration happens when the people redeemed by God's Son work together to accomplish the will of God the Father through the power of God's Spirit.
>
> **—James Harmeling, "Can We Work Together? A Biblical Theology of Collaboration"**

6. Review Paul's strategy for producing spiritual unity in Romans 15:14–16:27 as outlined in Burnett's essay. What are some strategic ways you can similarly encourage unity among members of the body of Christ in your current ministry context?

Missions Research

1. Research missionary attrition in missiological publications (blogs, magazines, journals, books), such as reported in the 1997 World Evangelical Fellowship Missions Committee's research project, and answer these questions.
a. What factors lead to missionaries leaving the field?

b. What are potential solutions to these problems?

c. How does unsolved conflict affect missionaries from the United States?

2. Compare and contrast the per capita income (PCI) of two different countries. How would a country with greater wealth create challenges and opportunities for the missionary? What about countries with lesser wealth? Is the claim true that missionaries make the biggest impact on the countries with the most money?

Figure 23.1

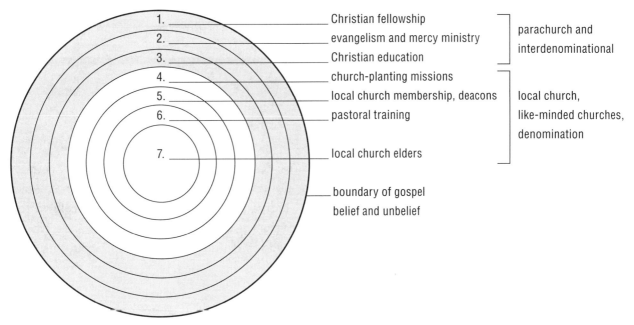

3. Use Cantrell's bull's-eye chart of collaboration in Figure 23.1 and choose one of the following items (Bible translation, orphan care, evangelistic event) for researching fruitful ministry partnerships, following the instructions.

BIBLE TRANSLATION

a. Research and list several Bible translation organizations and Bible societies that operate in a country or language group of your choosing.

b. Identify commonalities and contrasts in their core commitments and philosophies of ministry.

c. Defend which activities associated with Bible translation (per your research) should not be shared outside of like-minded evangelicals. Write each next to the appropriate level of Cantrell's bull's-eye chart in your understanding.

ORPHAN CARE

a. Research and list the responsibilities and activities of current Christian orphanages, particularly those in rural communities.

b. Label each listed item with the number of the ring of collaboration in which the responsibility is met or the activity is conducted.

c. State the role of local churches and supporting churches in the orphanages you researched, detailing how they collaborate, as far as you are able to observe.

EVANGELISTIC EVENT

a. Research several multiple-church evangelistic crusades in your country or in a different country, and list the main components of the events, including at least the following components: typical venues and locations; participating churches, including denomination names and theological identifiers (e.g., charismatic, Reformed); participating organizations, including ministry types (e.g., mercy ministry, publisher) and typical types of involvement (general attendance, speaking at the event, hosting a booth or table, etc.).

b. List the organizers' post-event follow-up strategies (one list for each crusade or, if essentially the same, one composite list), and label each item by the number of the ring of collaboration that is needed to accomplish the goal.

c. Identify any event activities and post-event strategies that seem to involve or encourage ministry partnerships that do not align with biblical teaching. State your reasons not to follow these partnership strategies.

Outside of the biblical gospel, there is no Christian fellowship, unity, or ministry partnership (2 Cor 6:14–18).

—Tim Cantrell, "Cooperation and Separation: Partnership in the Gospel Strategically and Selectively"

Application Projects

1. This project involves proposing and conducting a ministry partnership. Follow these steps to conscientiously form and faithfully carry out collaboration.

   a. Think of a ministry activity you would like to undertake with a partner, and list potential collaborators.

   b. Carefully consider Harmeling's six self-reflection questions regarding collaboration (listed here for convenience). Choose one potential collaborator with whom to discuss answers to some of the questions. Then reframe the questions appropriately for discussion, and answer them on a scale of 1 to 5, with 1 being "Absolutely Not," 3 being "Somewhat," and 5 being "Absolutely Yes."

   > ____ Are those I am considering working with committed to God's glory, or do they seek their own agenda and promotion?
   >
   > ____ Do we agree on essential points of doctrine? Do we agree on our definition of the gospel? Are there areas of disagreement on any theological point that causes concern?
   >
   > ____ Are the disagreements of doctrinal conviction in some areas significant enough to prevent collaboration on ministry efforts?
   >
   > ____ Do we agree on the direction and goal of the mission?
   >
   > ____ Do we agree on the methods, timing, and values used to accomplish the goal?
   >
   > ____ Do we agree on the roles each person or ministry plays in the project or in ongoing ministry endeavors?

   c. Together, prayerfully draft an action plan document for collaboration. Include answers to the following questions in your draft.

   > • What is the end goal, and do we agree on it?
   > • What is our path and process of achieving the end goal, and do we agree on it?
   > • What is each party's roles in accomplishing the end goal?
   > • Which steps does each party believe to be most vital in order to make progress?

   d. Decide on a milestone or date to assess the progress, spiritual health, and effectiveness of your partnership. Conduct team assessment using the following questions, and answer on a scale of 1 to 5, with 1 being "Absolutely Not," 3 being "Somewhat," and 5 being "Absolutely Yes."

   > ____ Are we faithfully meeting our responsibilities and finishing our portion of the work? Are we faithfully staying in communication when other parties rely on us for next steps?
   >
   > ____ Have we identified and resolved potential disagreements or divisions?
   >
   > ____ Do we understand significant cultural expressions, both verbal and nonverbal, that communicate caution, disagreement, confusion, or frustration?
   >
   > ____ Have we consistently restated positively the worth of what each person brings to the collaborative effort?

2. Identify two missionaries who have been partners on the mission field for at least several years. Write a letter to them together or request a joint interview to ask how they have maintained unity for so long. Ask if there have been any conflicts between them on the mission field that they are mutually willing to share and how they resolved them. Summarize their insights below.

3. Suppose a prospective missionary church planter approached your church seeking ongoing support. Create a list of requirements that must be met in order to consider such a partnership. What doctrinal distinctions must he hold to? How would you evaluate his character? What references would you require?

Best Practices for Effective Cultural Engagement

Textbook Content

CHAPTER 70: Fighting through the Fog: Exercising Discernment as a Missions Leader, by Mark Tatlock

> **INSERT 70.1:** Missionary Challenges in the MENA Region, by Hanna Shahin
>
> **INSERT 70.2:** An Open Letter to Hindu Christ Followers, by Daniel Surya Avula

CHAPTER 71: Toward a Biblical Model of Cultural Engagement, by Chris Burnett

> **INSERT 71.1:** Too Cultured? Hyper-contextualization in Asia Today, by E. D. Burns
>
> **INSERT 71.2:** Marketplace Ministry: A Natural Approach to Disciple-Making, by Peter Olivetan
>
> **INSERT 71.3:** Marketplace Ministry: The "10x" Factor, by L. C. Ridley

CHAPTER 72: Ten Mistakes Missionaries Make, by Cecil Stalnaker

> **INSERT 72.1:** Building Cultural Intelligence in Pre-field Missions Training, by Lisa LaGeorge
>
> **INSERT 72.2:** A Biblical Framework for Shalom Today, by William D. Barrick
>
> **INSERT 72.3:** *Ethos* before *Logos*: Acts 18 as a Case Study, by David Beakley

Key Memory Verse

See to it that no one takes you captive through philosophy and empty deception, according to the tradition of men, according to the elementary principles of the world, and not according to Christ.

—COLOSSIANS 2:8

Additional Memory Verses

- Isaiah 52:7
- 1 Corinthians 2:1–5
- 2 Corinthians 10:3–6
- Ephesians 6:12
- Colossians 1:13

Scriptures for Further Meditation

- Jeremiah 29:7; Isaiah 53:5; Acts 17:11; Romans 1:21; 8:7; 1 Corinthians 9:19–23; 2 Corinthians 2:14–17; 1 Thessalonians 1:9–10; 2:13

Summary of Textbook Content

As the missionary battles with a host of competing worldviews and philosophies, the truth is his only true weapon. Yet he cannot wield it with precision unless he knows what to combat. Thus, the missionary must not only have a clear grasp on sound doctrine, but he must have the discernment necessary to wisely navigate the false systems of thought and the worldly methods he encounters. He must resist the worldly wisdom that aims to make the truth palatable to a target audience. Rather, the missionary's message is inherently confrontational as he exposes error and calls people to biblical repentance and sanctification. At the same time, cultural awareness is critical if the missionary is to ensure the message alone is offensive and not his own personal conduct. It is only when the missionary himself is out of the way that the gospel may go forth with clarity. The missionary's deep credibility with his audience comes only from strong cultural awareness, extensive language acquisition, and genuine concern for the welfare of those around him. With an *ethos* that strong, the *logos* may go forth unimpeded.

Learning Objectives

- Develop discernment for evaluating unbiblical worldviews and worldly missions methods.

- Identify key components of cultural intelligence (CQ) needed for cross-cultural adaptation.
- Acquire a model of cross-cultural communication that is faithful to biblical priorities.
- Recognize the importance of language acquisition in effective missions efforts.
- Understand the correct place of cultural **contextualization** in missions.
- Explain the importance of credibility (*ethos*) for effective gospel communication (*logos*).
- Comprehend what it means to seek the shalom of those around you and how to apply it in practical ways abroad.

> Effective CQ is an essential skill for any Christian for three primary reasons: each individual comes from a culture, the Church is multicultural, and reading the Scriptures is a cross-cultural activity.
>
> —**Chris Burnett, "Toward a Biblical Model of Cultural Engagement"**

Recall and Reflect

1. According to Tatlock, what are the tools needed for discernment, and what Scriptures support this claim? [Tatlock, "Fighting through the Fog"]

2. What are the consequences of failing to teach a correct bibliology to a new convert? [Tatlock, "Fighting through the Fog"]

3. What did Shahin say are the primary hindrances to the gospel in the MENA region? [Shahin, "Missionary Challenges in the MENA Region"]

4. Summarize the approach of the Hindu Christ followers movement. What are the four flaws that Avula identifies with this movement? [Avula, "An Open Letter to Hindu Christ Followers"]

5. What are the three parameters of a biblical model of cultural engagement? List and summarize each. [Burnett, "Toward a Biblical Model of Cultural Engagement"]

6. What examples of contextualization does Burns present in his article? How have these practices hindered the growth of the church in Asia? [Burns, "Too Cultured?"]

7. Define and contrast the "Platform Model" and the "Marketplace Ministry Model," and tell how each has influenced missionary work. [Ridley, "Marketplace Ministry"]

8. According to Stalnaker, what are the four main activities from which missionaries are tempted to drift? [Stalnaker, "Ten Mistakes Missionaries Make"]

9. Describe the following Greek terms: *logos*, *ethos*, and *pathos*. Why is it important that a missionary utilize all three? What are the consequences of failing to be consistent in any one of these modes of persuasion? [Beakley, *Ethos* before *Logos*]

Analyze

1. Why should churches exercise greater discernment regarding the missionary agencies that they choose for partnership?

2. What is the relationship between culture and worldview? Based on this understanding, why is it misguided for missionaries to focus on changing the culture? What should they be focusing on instead, and why?

3. Explain why someone in a hostile context cannot continue following their old religious practices when they come to faith in Christ. Use Scripture to support your answer.

4. Why is the missionary's task confrontational in nature? Is confrontation avoidable in true biblical missions? Why or why not?

5. How might the "biblical missions model" of cultural engagement be important to understand when counseling someone? How would this help the missionary in the aim of maturing disciples and equipping them for ministry?

6. How would a missionary's efforts look different if he focused on biblical disciple-making rather than on achieving large numbers of converts?

7. What are the situations in which marketplace ministry is most effective, and why?

8. What is the 10/40 window, and what is its significance for missions?

9. Do you agree with Stalnaker's assessment that missionaries must work hard at being good theologians? Why?

10. What are some of the dangers of heading to the field with false motivations?

Implement

1. What steps can you take to guard against what Stalnaker calls "mission drift"?

2. How might you go about establishing *ethos* as a missionary in a foreign culture?

3. What can you learn from the Marketplace Ministry Model, and how might this apply in your current context?

4. How can you pray this week for the people of the MENA region and the missionaries serving there in light of challenges discussed by Shahin?

> The mission of the church in the world is clear: biblically trained believers must go and confront the false beliefs and evil practices of every culture. They do this by confrontationally asserting the content of Scripture and discipling all regenerate believers toward God-glorifying maturity.
>
> —Chris Burnett, "Toward a Biblical Model of Cultural Engagement"

5. What can your church do to help combat competing ideologies that are propagated in local universities?

6. What are some ways that you have seen the church attempt to change the culture without affecting the heart? What has been the outcome of such efforts?

7. How does the fact that God's Word can be accurately understood and faithfully applied in a different language and cultural context motivate you to engage in biblical proclamation? What do you think missionary activities would look like without this confidence?

Ask a Missionary

1. Which unbiblical worldviews have made disciple-making difficult in the country you serve? How have you attempted to overcome those hurdles?

2. In what ways have you been tempted to deviate from your mission, and how have you avoided doing so? How have you course corrected when necessary?

3. What cultural habits or practices did you have to abandon to establish greater credibility among the people you serve?

4. How has discernment aided you on the mission field? Describe a time when discernment protected you.

5. With the experience you've gained on the mission field, what would you do differently if you were to start again?

6. Have you ever followed the Marketplace Ministry Model in your local context? If so, what did your day-to-day life as a missionary look like?

7. For marketplace ministers in the 10/40 window: What opportunities for the gospel have you encountered at your job? What challenges do you face in proclaiming the gospel? How do you attempt to navigate those challenges?

Study the Scriptures

1. Read through 1 Corinthians 2 and contrast the principles of man's wisdom with God's wisdom. Speculate what missiology would look like if based on man's wisdom? What would it look like if based on God's wisdom?

2. Read Ephesians 6:17. What is significant about "the word of God" (i.e., "the sword of the Spirit") being both an offensive and a defensive weapon? How can missionaries employ the Word of God in both offensive and defensive ways?

3. What categories of thinking does Paul warn against in Colossians 2:8? Study what Paul means by each of these concepts, using an exegetical or background commentary on the passage. How should the missionary be aware of the warning contained in this passage for himself or herself today?

4. Read John 3:21 and 1 John 1:6. What is the difference between aligning one's theology with truth (orthodoxy) and practicing the truth (orthopraxy)? Why must a missionary be expected to do both?

5. Read 1 Corinthians 4:1–7 closely. How are the concepts of *ethos* and *pathos* addressed by Paul in this passage?

Missings Research

1. Research the spiritual beliefs, traditions, and practices of a country or region known for embracing a false religion or for operating according to a false worldview (e.g., Hinduism in Bali, Indonesia; Buddhism in Myanmar; animism in Cameroon; naturalistic atheism in Albania). In the following chart, list at least ten observations of the beliefs, concepts, customs, and practices of the false worldview. Then devise a list of spiritual problems that correspond specifically to each of your observations.

Observation	Spiritual Problem
Example: Traditional healers in Sierra Leone sprinkle chicken blood on the ailing body parts of sick patients to cure them from what is perceived as curses by evil spirits.	Desperate people are deceived and distracted by evil leaders so that they will not seek spiritual deliverance by Christ.
1.	
2.	
3.	
4.	
5.	
6.	
7.	
8.	
9.	
10.	

2. Identify the most influential false worldview of a country you are interested in serving or currently serve, and do the following tasks:

   a. Describe the beliefs, concepts, customs, and practices that stem from the false worldview you have identified.

   b. Describe three examples of how this false worldview might (or does) creep into the beliefs and practices of some form of Christianity there (including evangelical churches, Roman Catholicism, liberal Christianity, or others).

   c. For each of these examples, explain at least one problem it creates for missionaries who desire to preach the gospel and teach theology to local people caught up in such syncretism.

3. Study the biography of a faithful missionary of your choosing from the past.

   Figure 24.1

   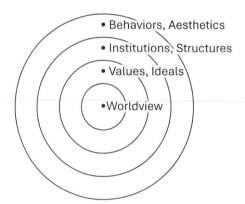

   a. How was the model of culture shown in Figure 24.1 manifested at each layer in your chosen missionary's field context? (For example, a worldview that prized power led to values demonstrating patriarchal dominance, to institutions that subjugated women and children, and to behaviors of human trafficking and abuse.)

   b. List how the culture, even if at a contained local level, changed from the inside outward at each level because of the gospel's entrance through the missionary.

Biblical Missions Model

I. PREPARATION

A. Learn.
1. Learn conservative evangelical doctrine.
2. Learn original language exegesis.
3. Learn text-driven exegetical theological method.
4. Learn target language.

B. Practice.
1. Practice historical, grammatical hermeneutics.
2. Practice text-driven exegetical theological method.
3. Practice expository preaching.

C. Observe.
1. Observe cultural customs and practices.
2. Seek to understand worldview and beliefs.
3. Seek to understand customs and practices.

II. PROCLAMATION

A. Evangelize the people.
1. (Involve an interpreter until language proficiency.)
2. (Translate Scripture if needed.)
3. Confront sins and false beliefs.
4. Preach the gospel.

B. Preach expository sermons.
1. Regularly assemble believers for the preaching event.
2. Prefer Bible books to topics.

C. Teach expositionally in the local church.
1. Regularly assemble believers for Bible study.
2. Instill regular Bible-reading behaviors.
3. Train believers in hermeneutics, including basic native linguistic analysis.
4. Guide to determine text's meaning and intentions (implications).
5. Guide to propose possible applications.
6. Guide to evaluate customs and practices of the church.

D. Identify maturing disciples in the local church.
1. Conduct full-immersion water baptism.
2. Encourage formal church membership.
3. Observe responsiveness to teaching and progressive sanctification.
4. Encourage ministry participation.

E. **Train leaders for the local church.**
  1. Train in biblical exposition.
  2. Train in expository preaching.
  3. Train in pastoral ministry.
  4. Train to apply Scripture to mature in holiness and to avoid syncretism.
     a. In the life of the believers (personal, family, daily life).
     b. In the life of the church (worship, ministries).
     c. In the witness of the church to the world (evangelism, outreach).
  5. Train to plant new local churches.

Application Projects

1. Ask a missionary to provide you with an example of a conflict they encountered on the mission field. Ask them also to omit the manner in which they resolved the issue. Exercise discernment and, in your own words, describe below how you would respond to that particular issue. Afterward, discuss with the missionary the conflict, the missionary's own resolution, and, if different, what they believe the biblical resolution to have been. Record insights gained or modifications you would make after your discussion.

2. Think of a friend or family member who professes faith in Christ but seems to live no differently from the rest of the world. Write a letter expressing your concern for the genuineness of their faith, explaining with Scripture what it means to be a Christian. Urge them in a loving way to "walk in the Light, as He Himself is in the light" (1 John 1:7). Then, prayerfully either send them the letter or plan to discuss those truths with them in your next conversation.

3. Choose a country with a language you do not currently know. Respond to the prompts with the Biblical Missions Model of cultural engagement that precedes this list. You might benefit from interviewing one or more missionaries who serve or have served there as you answer.
   a. What specific activities might you undertake to accomplish the bulleted components of step I.C? Provide a range of practical ideas with many details, including a list of websites and print resources to which you referred for ideas.

b. Report the perceived cultural elements, sins, and false beliefs of the target audience that might make step II.A difficult to achieve. Be specific about each item you list, and provide a brief explanation for each.

c. Propose the duration of time it might take to complete steps I.A, B, and C in years and months. Write the time frame to the right of each list item.

d. Which three to five items listed in part II most excite you to accomplish on the target field? Rank them by desire, placing numbers to the left of the items, with number 1 being the activity you most look forward to doing. Provide brief explanations for your rankings.

The spiritual battlefield is made perilous by unbiblical philosophies that cloud and confuse modern-day missions, philosophies that ultimately inhibit the missionary's ability to achieve the missional obligations of the New Testament. Therefore, those going into the battle must cultivate biblical discernment in order to fight through the fog of extrabiblical philosophies and not be taken captive.

—Mark Tatlock, "Fighting through the Fog: Exercising Discernment as a Missions Leader"

Take your next steps at
TMAI.ORG/BIBLICAL-MISSIONS

THE CENTER FOR
BILICAL MISSIONS
at TMAI

Equipping the global church
for effective biblical missions

The Center for Biblical Missions at TMAI seeks to produce and house scripturally based resources to equip believers for global missions in every region of the world.

CONTENT

Access biblical resources for your ongoing education

- Videos from the authors
- Field documentaries
- Online courses
- Downloadable articles & study guides

CONSULTING

Engage with missions leaders to shape your strategy

- Expert guidance from trusted ministry partners in our network
- Personalized consultations
- Missions strategy development

CONNECTING

Network with our missions-minded community

- Supportive relationships for local churches & missions leaders
- Missions conferences
- Short-term opportunities & internships

THE
**MASTER'S ACADEMY
INTERNATIONAL**

The Master's Academy International (TMAI) is a non-profit organization that has been committed to fulfilling the Great Commission by training indigenous church leaders to be approved pastor-teachers, able to equip their churches to make biblically sound disciples.

Partner With Us

INTERCEDE
Prayer is still our greatest need today. We invite you to join us in praying for the Lord's work through TMAI around the world. Sign up for prayer updates at *tmai.org/subscribe*.

INVEST
Our ministry would not be possible without the generosity of our donors. If you are interested in financially supporting this exciting global work, visit *tmai.org/donate*.

INTRODUCE
You can play a significant role in TMAI's ministry by introducing us to others who share a passion to see Christ's name exalted among the nations. Email us at *info@tmai.org*.

Our Schools

Albania | Argentina | Croatia | Czech Republic | Germany | Honduras | India
Italy | Japan | Malawi | Mexico | Myanmar | Middle East | Russia | South Africa
Spain | The Philippines | Ukraine | United States (Russian-Speakers)

Learn More

TMAI.ORG · 818.909.5570 · INFO@TMAI.ORG